a
HANDFUL
of
HAPPINESS

a HANDFUL of HAPPINESS

How a Prickly Creature
Softened a Prickly Heart

MASSIMO VACCHETTA
WITH ANTONELLA TOMASELLI
(TRANSLATION BY JAMIE RICHARDS)

RODALE.

Translation copyright © 2018 by Penguin Random House LLC
Copyright © 2016 by Sperling & Kupfer Editori S.P.A.

Published in the United States by Rodale Books,
an imprint of the Crown Publishing Group, a division of
Penguin Random House LLC, New York.

crownpublishing.com
rodalebooks.com

RODALE and the Plant colophon are registered trademarks of
Penguin Random House LLC.

This work was originally published in Italian as
25 Grammi Di Felicita by Sperling & Kupfer Editori S.P.A.,
an imprint of Mondadori Libri S.P.A., in 2016.

Library of Congress Cataloging-in-Publication Data is
available upon request.

ISBN 978–1–63565–264–2
Ebook ISBN 978-1-63565-265-9

PRINTED IN THE UNITED STATES OF AMERICA

Book design by Yeon Kim
Jacket design by Yeon Kim
Jacket photograph by Nature Picture Library/Alamy Stock Photo

10 9 8 7 6 5 4 3 2 1

First U.S. Edition

INTRODUCTION

The pages ahead tell a story that's true to its core: the story of Massimo Vacchetta and his hedgehogs. I met Massimo by chance—though who knows, maybe nothing happens purely by chance—and immediately wanted to write about him. About his hedgehog world and La Ninna Hedgehog Rescue Center. I wrote a two-page feature for a weekly magazine I contribute to called *Confidenze tra amiche.* The response was enthusiastic.

Then came a request from publisher Sperling & Kupfer: "Can we make this into a book?" And here it is. Massimo told me everything over hours, days, weeks, and months on the telephone. As he talked, he looked after his hedgehogs—our phone conversations did not distract him from their care for a single minute. I, on the other hand, just listened attentively, so as not to miss anything. Even to the words he did not say. And especially his feelings, in all their light and shadow, so as to convey them to you, the reader. Trying not to use a filter of my own. I tried my best, but sometimes the heart, in secret, slips in, and you don't even notice.

Like him, I have loved animals since I was little. My husband and my son have, too. We have four dogs: Luna, Mare, Blu, and Mostrilla. And a ginger cat who comes to visit us every day. Charmed, we always welcome him with open arms. His name is Pimky. We also have fifteen goldfish in a pond we built ourselves. Some frogs have made homes there, and their croaking fills the air every summer.

We've never seen hedgehogs in our garden, but we're sure they come out and scamper around at night.

But back to Massimo. If every person on this earth is unique, Massimo is a little bit more so. Between one story and the next, I found myself thinking he would never grow old. He has the soul of a poet and the eyes of a child. That's why he sees beauty even where others do not. That's the way he is, as you are about to read. Sentimental and a dreamer. With his mistakes and faults, which he doesn't hide. With his regrets. With his sorrows. With his joys. With his insecurities and his convictions. And with his desires to do and to give, which are irrepressible. At least as long as there are hedgehogs forgotten by the world that need him. At least as long as he lives.

Antonella Tomaselli

1

May 2013. Spring was in full swing, yet it was passing me by. Its sights and scents seemed faded and far away. I was lost.

An urgent need for change was burning inside me. My desire to pursue a new dream hadn't waned. Despite everything. Despite the wounds I'd borne and battles I'd lost.

I brushed my hair off my forehead, as if to push away those intense thoughts, and opened my closet. Matching colors with meticulous care, I picked out a pair of pants, a light turtleneck, a blazer, shoes, socks. I added a nice watch. Dressed to the nines, I looked in the mirror. Everything was right, down to the last detail. I went into the living room. Greta was there, curled up on the sofa. She looked up from her tablet.

"You look nice," she said, pleased.

As she looked at me, her bright expression faded. "But your eyes always have a little sadness. Even when you smile," she added, almost whispering.

I let out a little sigh in response.

"I'll be back soon," I said and, grabbing the car keys, went out. I drove slowly through traffic, while sensations and reflections alternated and intermingled in my mind. I was dissatisfied with my work and with my life. I felt like I was groping my way through a dark, empty room, with nothing to orient me. I needed something I could get excited about. Something that would give me the desire to live that I was hungry for. Greta pushed me, thinking she was being helpful. But I didn't want to go in the direction she suggested. It was hers, not mine.

I decided to become a veterinarian as soon as I graduated high school. To everyone around me, even me, it seemed like a random choice. But it wasn't. I only realized later that it had deep roots in my childhood. Maybe I was simply born with a desire to help animals. Who knows.

All the same, after years of doing that job, there I was, feeling like something wasn't right anymore. Something was missing. A great absence whose weight I could feel without knowing its name.

Greta had insisted pragmatically: "Try doing something different. For example, you could start working with small animals. Dogs, cats. All pets. You'd earn a lot more, you know.

And you need to think about retirement. An extra pension. Or life insurance." It was like talking to my father: Do this, do that. But that's not how I was or am. I'm the opposite of someone who plans out his life. It wasn't my style. I couldn't see myself closed inside a clinic going back and forth between vaccinations and microchips. I was used to different situations, more extreme ones.

But.

Following her advice, I'd started working at two small animal clinics. Just a couple of times a week. I was on my way to one that day—I had to take over for Andrea, the owner, for the weekend. When I got there, after saying hello, he launched into all the instructions. He explained everything there was to do as we exchanged banter about ourselves and work. Before we parted ways, he showed me a box. Inside was a little animal. It was tiny.

"It's a baby hedgehog," he said.

I looked at the little creature, curious.

"A woman found it in her garden. It's an orphan," Andrea continued. "She brought it here because she didn't know what to do with it."

The little thing still had its eyes closed. And pink, hairless skin. The spines were white and soft, a bit disheveled. They started just behind his tiny ears and ran all the way down his back.

"It was born two or three days ago. It weighs less than an ounce—only twenty-five grams," Andrea said.

"Twenty-five grams is nothing," I remarked.

"Yeah. You'll have to feed it several times."

"Which milk is the best substitute for its mother's?"

"I was recommended goat's milk. Cow's milk doesn't work because it has a very high level of lactose, a sugar that hedge-hogs don't tolerate well. You'll have to feed it by syringe, one drop at a time."

"How unusual!"

I took the hedgehog and set it on the palm of my hand, to observe it more closely. I paused to look at its front paws: Its slender toes made them look like little hands. I was struck by that similarity. But, pushing away the sentimentality that was starting to wash over me, I suggested to Andrea, smiling, "Let's take some pictures of him and put them on Facebook."

We took a number of selfies with our smartphones. Me, him, and the baby hedgehog. Me and the hedgehog. Him and the hedgehog. We chose the best ones to post. We said good-bye. And I went back home, where Greta was waiting for me.

The next morning, I got ready with my usual care. I put on a pair of jeans and a blue linen button-down. I went through my jackets and chose one that was casual yet impeccably cut. Light tan color. Paired it with loafers. I checked myself thoroughly in the mirror. My physical appearance was important to me. I was aware of having a certain appeal, and I cultivated it.

As arranged, I went to Andrea's clinic. I wanted to see to the hedgehog again. That odd little creature had gotten to me the day before. I opened the door and stood there, frozen. It was whimpering. A soft, small whimper. Like a chick. A baby bird. A constant, tiny wail broken up by brief pauses. It went straight to the heart. It stung. It hurt. A tear-shaped sound, faint yet shrill.

The little hedgehog was crying for help.

I approached the box filled with wood shavings where it was contained. I took the critter out and set it on the nearby table.

The hedgehog was cold. It was the chill of life slipping away, moving aside for death. I felt infinite sorrow for that little animal. I was assailed by feelings that were familiar to me yet new, as if they'd been roused from a slumber that had kept them hidden or trapped for ages. I was accustomed to animals in pain. I had built a shield around myself that allowed me a certain detachment. That shield shattered at the sight of that creature.

I looked at the urchin with new eyes. I saw how it was an orphan. I imagined its mother getting hit by a car while searching for food. Maybe flattened on the asphalt. Or left incapable of returning to her den in another horrible way. I imagined the baby, waiting in vain. And its fear. Probably, desperate, it had emerged from its nest to search for its mother. And in an instant, like a thunderbolt, I felt its solitude. Complete. Boundless. I recognized it. It was like mine, mine as a child.

2

My maternal grandparents had played a significant role in my childhood. They lived in the country. They were farmers. Two easygoing, supportive people. Arms to take refuge in.

I often stayed with them, especially during school holidays, because my parents worked. Nonna Caterina was simple. Transparent as glass. She was goodness itself. A limited culture and a certain degree of illiteracy, mixed with the mentality of that era and those places, didn't stifle her gentle ways and beauty. Sometimes she took me with her to the stable. I was little, and she'd put me in a basket. She sat next to me and knitted while telling me stories. I listened. And watched the cows and calves. And the swallows that had their nests there in droves.

When I was a little older, I'd go with her to the fields, trying to help her out. After, we would head for the row of trees at the edge of the yard. We sat on the grass, in the shade. She'd pull out lunch or a snack from the basket she'd brought along. We ate, enveloped in the scent of hay. And all was calm. Sometimes we fell asleep to the soundtrack of crickets and cicadas, making the slow rhythms of the country, those days, that season, our own.

My grandfather was an extraordinary character. He never raised his voice, yet he was resolute, even tough at times. A man of the country, of the utmost integrity and a sharp mind. He always kept his head firmly on his shoulders. And he put it to good use. He was calm on the inside and dynamic on the outside. Active. He had an asthma problem, and his breath was accompanied by a constant wheeze. After three steps, he'd have to stop for a moment, to catch his breath. It was an enormous issue that he tolerated well but didn't want to be too affected by. My father, who was fixated on medicine, was always there to give him his inhaler, to take care of him. He'd say, "I'm extending his life." And it was true: It was of great help to him. At my grandparents' house, there was also Osvaldo, my mother's youngest brother. Not just my uncle, he was a brother to me too. A big brother. At the end of summer, I would go back home with Mama and Papa. Our farewells were like a funeral. Nonna cried. So did I.

Yet I encountered loneliness even with my grandparents. Absence. My father and mother often stopped by to see me in the evening. I waited for them. The moment darkness fell, I would plant myself at the kitchen window, standing virtually still. My eyes anxiously scanned the headlights of every approaching car. I waited in silence. I missed my mom. A lot.

Back home in the fall, I returned to school. I attended a parochial school run by nuns. At the sound of the bell, all the children would be off, squealing and laughing as they headed for home. Only I stayed. Long, interminable afternoons. Until four-thirty or five when my mom came to get me. At school I waited at the window, too. The hours were endless. I was all alone. I often drew. Sister Francesca told me I was good. Each time she looked at my drawings, an "oh" of wonder was stamped on her face.

If it was nice out, I was allowed to wait in the school court-yard. It was all right. There was a garden at the end. I rode around on my bicycle. Back and forth. And in circles. Forward, backward, and around. Sometimes I would stop, one foot resting on the ground, the other still on the pedal, to look at a butterfly. Or I'd drop the bike and chase a lizard. I watched ants and other insects I couldn't name. Every day the same, with the fear that my mom wouldn't come. Ever.

Then she'd appear. I ran to meet her. She smiled. She took me in her arms. She put me on her bike seat and pushed it while walking. That's how we would go home while we talked about our day. In June, classes ended. But my parents didn't take me to my grandparents' right away. I stayed at school until it was completely closed for the summer. I was the only child who stayed. I spent all day riding my BMX in the courtyard. Forward, backward, around, and past the horse chestnuts.

I was always terrified of losing her, my mom. I'd absorbed this fear from my father: He was a hypochondriac, and his topics of conversation often revolved around sickness and death. Every day he came out with a new one. "I'm sure I have cancer. I won't make it to thirty," he'd declare. I was little. In time I understood his problem. But not then. I believed he was really going to die by age thirty. I was filled with sadness. I drew in his anxieties all the time. They inevitably became my own, and I projected them onto my mother. And then Dad and Mom didn't get along. They threatened to separate. It was terrible for me. I was scared of losing them. Yes, I was going to lose them to divorce or to illness. One of the two. There was no avoiding it. And my child's heart was frightened. My childhood was shadowed by this fear of abandonment. By absence. By loneliness.

There, at Andrea's clinic that Saturday morning, watching the little hedgehog cry, I instantly understood his fears, his desperation. Because I knew them myself.

3

That little animal no longer had anyone in the world. There was just me to help him. For the first time in my life, I found myself talking to a hedgehog. "I won't abandon you, little one. I won't leave you here in this box to die of cold and hunger. I'll do everything in my power to save you."

I had to think fast. First, it was crucial to get him to recover some body heat, so I filled a hot water bottle with warm water and put it beside him. Then I rushed over to my laptop. I wanted more specific information. I didn't know a thing about hedgehogs, except four or five basic notions. I started to search online. I found a forum about them. The contact was someone named Giulia. I called her, but there was no answer. Once, twice, three times. Nothing.

Worry.

Finally she answered. I showered her with a river of words, one after the other virtually without pause: "Giulia my name is Massimo I have a baby hedgehog that weighs twenty-five grams I found it yesterday we're giving it goat's milk but I have the impression that it's not doing well"—tiny pause for half-breath—"now the little thing seems very cold I think it needs some kind of treatment but I don't know what help me."

Her sweet voice and placid tone seemed to exist for the sole purpose of calming my nerves. She began to speak, softly yet precisely: "Well, your intuition is right, goat's milk isn't ideal. It's hydrating but not nutritious enough, you know. Mama hedgehog milk is much more concentrated, with lots of protein and fat and almost no sugar. You should give him puppy formula. Not just any one. There are only two good kinds. Neither is the same as its mother's milk, but they're better than goat. Get one of those."

"Where can I find them?"

"Lots of pet stores. Even some drugstores."

"Okay. And how do I administer it? With an insulin syringe? A miniature bottle?"

"An insulin syringe is fine. You have to make sure the milk doesn't go the wrong way. The hoglet could die from aspiration pneumonia. You have to give it to him very slowly. Then you have to massage his genital area to stimulate his bowels. That's what his mother would do. You have to take care of him like she would. But since you're not a hedgehog"—she paused for a second, for a little laugh—"take a little soft cloth or, better yet, a cotton round, the kind for taking makeup off. Put a little almond oil on it, wrap it around your finger, and massage him softly. It's essential. In their first three weeks of life, approximately, hedgehogs are unable empty their intestines or bladders on their own, and if you don't help them, they can get a dangerous blockage."

Giulia went on further, until she had gone through all the primary information. That was the only time we spoke. Later on, our contact, although frequent, was just by e-mail and text.

After hanging up, I started searching the Internet for pet stores, warehouses, and drugstores. I made more calls than I could count, but the puppy formula Giulia had recommended was nowhere. Some I asked had never even heard of it. Finally, a supplier in Florence told me that he could get it, but it wouldn't arrive until the following Wednesday.

"There's no way to get it faster?" I begged.

"It's Saturday. I can't put in the order before Monday morning. I'll send it by courier. There's nothing more I can do."

I sighed, resigned. Nothing left to do but wait.

Meanwhile I'd go on with goat's milk, perhaps slightly increasing the number of feedings.

I took the baby and brought him home. Greta welcomed me, curious.

As I was telling her the whole story, I got a cardboard box, put a soft towel on the bottom, and set the little thing inside.

But first I weighed him again: still twenty-five grams. Well, at least he hadn't lost weight. I put a fresh hot water bottle next to him. I wanted to give him a blanket, but Greta objected: "No, that's too much. You'll suffocate him!" I listened to her, mostly because I didn't want to waste time. I had to give the creature some milk. I took a butterfly needle, the kind for an IV, and cut the tip from the connector on the syringe to the needle down to a centimeter, which made it into a sort of tiny nipple. I removed the needle, attached the nipple to the syringe, and drew in the milk.

Giulia had explained to me how to hold the hoglet while I fed him. I set him on the table, holding him down with my left hand so he had his front legs extended and back legs flexed. "Like a dog on its back with its head up, just to give you an idea," she added.

I placed a finger on either side of his neck, gingerly, to keep him from turning side to side. With my right hand, I brought the syringe to his mouth. I fed him the milk drop by drop, following his pace, with extreme care: one drop, pause to swallow, another drop. I didn't want it to go the wrong way. I was also aware of the danger of aspiration pneumonia—it's very serious and nearly always fatal. I pushed the plunger of the syringe, giving him 0.1 cc at a time. It couldn't be easy for the hedgehog to have a rubber nub in his mouth instead of his mother's nipple. But it was hard for me, too. My hands were used to big animals and 150 mL syringes.

It took me a good twenty minutes to feed him. I continued taking care of him, following Giulia's instructions to the letter, while Greta looked on in astonishment. She, too, was touched and fascinated by the unusual and fragile little animal.

Then I went back to Andrea's clinic to finish the work that had to be done there, interspersing it with trips home to take care of the hedgehog. The day went by in a flash. I had an unusual night ahead of me: I had to set my alarm for every two or three hours, because with such young babies, you have to follow that schedule to feed them.

Sunday morning around eight, after having given the hedgehog yet another syringe of goat's milk, I realized that I didn't even feel that tired, despite my practically sleepless night. Maybe my desire to help the little creature was so great it canceled out the toil and fatigue. Just a shower and it was back to the zigzag between home and Andrea's clinic. First thing after lunch, I weighed the hoglet: twenty-four grams. His weight had dropped. By a gram. Despite my efforts.

I felt utterly sad and powerless. I was worried. I started weighing him before and after every feeding. My worry turned into obsession. I was afraid for his life. I had another busy night. Just after three, I fell asleep like a rock, a deep sleep. At six, when the alarm went off, I felt like I had only closed my eyes for a second, even though almost three hours had gone by. Once again: weigh, give goat's milk, reweigh, massage, hot water bottle. I wanted to go back to bed, but it was Monday—I had to go to work.

I specialized in bovines. Gynecology and obstetrics were my forte, delivery my passion. And at this time of year, there were lots of calves about to be born. How could I look after a birthing cow and feed the baby hedgehog every three hours? I couldn't ask Greta. She only stayed with me on the weekends, then went back to her own place and work. I hopped in the shower. The water flowing over me woke me up. I hastily put on the first clothes I came across—as was *not* my habit!—and rushed out of the house. I didn't even bother to look in the mirror. I'd gotten a call from a breeder, a client of mine. What I had been afraid of had come true: There was a laboring cow in distress . . . a good distance away.

4

I reached the farm very quickly. But once I got there, I realized I wouldn't be able to handle the rest so fast. Certainly not within the measured window of time I had before the hedgehog's next feeding.

My client was an expert breeder. He had already tried to help the mother and child, with no appreciable results. The calf was in breech position. And it was huge. A not-good yet not-new situation, but in this case, it was rather dramatic. It was stuck inside its mother's pelvis. I palpated its legs: cold. And, unfortunately, not moving either. The little one could already be dead. I had to act effectively and quickly. My adrenaline was pumping.

I immediately asked for some oil to lubricate the birth canal and make it easier to push the calf out. With the help of the breeder and a few of his workers, we tied the calf's back legs together with two thick cotton laces and attached them to a big hemp rope. In a desperate battle against time, I instructed the others, "At my signal, pull the rope until I tell you to stop. Then just hold it in place. You'll start pulling again at my next signal."

We got started. I signaled in rhythm with the mother's contractions. The two men at the other end of the rope followed my orders with zeal and attention. Sometimes they slipped, but they planted their feet in the ground again. They wore themselves out, yet the situation didn't improve. The poor cow was tired, as were those who were helping her unsuccessfully. But I hadn't given up yet.

Trying to solve the problem, I pressed on the calf's pelvis, trying to rotate it. Around the same time, the cow started pushing again. "Pull! Pull!" I cried excitedly. We heard something like a crack. An instant later, the two men holding the rope stumbled, almost falling backward. And the calf was out of the mother. There it was! But there was no time to stop and smile: The little one was limp. He wasn't breathing, but his heart was beating. I immediately injected him with medication and held him upside down to increase the bloodflow to the brain and free the airways of fluid. At the same time, I pushed his front legs out to extend his rib cage and aid ventilation.

But the calf was unresponsive.

I put him on the ground. "Bring me some cold water," I

shouted. I threw it on his ears, on his head, to try and rouse him. But it got no reaction.

His little head dangled. Atonic. I tried giving him "mouth to nose." I blew into one of his nostrils while holding the other closed to dilate his lungs.

It didn't work. I sank down, exhausted and resigned. Nothing and no one moved in that stable. Everyone had their head bowed in the face of death. A few seconds went by . . . and then the heavy silence was broken by a kind of sucking sound.

I knew that sound well.

I spun around. The calf had let out a breath. He was alive. I went back to resuscitating him, until his breathing became regular. Then we brought him over to his mother, who started licking him affectionately. There, he was safe and sound. But I didn't have time to enjoy the sight that, despite twenty years in the profession, always filled me with wonder. Now it was time to take care of the hoglet. I had to get to him fast. I'd gone a little past the interval between meals.

I found him asleep. He woke up just as I put him in my hand to give him his milk. Then the phone rang. It was my client, the breeder. I put him on speakerphone: "Doctor, everything's okay! The calf is happily drinking milk from his mama!"

There it was. At the same time, a twenty-five-gram hedgehog was drinking a single drop of milk while a forty-kilo calf was gulping it down.

Life.

I was happy.

Monday went by to the rhythm of my back-and-forth from bovines to hedgehog and back. Same on Tuesday. Identical and intense days.

Giulia told me that I could let more time pass between the hoglet's nighttime feedings. But with the contingencies and urgency of my work, I couldn't plan and it was hard for me to stick to three hours between the little one's feedings. I decided I would make up for it by rigorously respecting that interval during the night. I preferred to sacrifice my sleep.

Within a few days, my physical appearance had changed. And not for the better. But for the first time, I didn't really care. Over the years, I'd come to place enormous importance on my external appearance, concerning myself far too much with the human side.

Zia Marilena noticed. She wasn't really my aunt, even though I called her that. She was a cousin from my father's side. A very intelligent and logical woman, she had assumed an important role in my life early on. She gave me advice, and helped me to analyze some of my behaviors and to accept myself. She suffered from severe scoliosis. But she bore her conspicuous hunch with nonchalance. To her, those things did not matter. She told me: "Massimo, it's true, you're a little nar-cissistic, but it's because you're insecure. You take refuge in your handsome, put-together look. Or you hide behind it. It makes you feel safe, and so you put all your focus on that, but it's so empty, ephemeral. You have much more to offer. And if I say so, you can believe it."

Was she right? When I opened up to her, I was able to dig up my buried anxieties.

The fact is, besides my fear of abandonment, of separation, that had brought me so much suffering as a child, there was also my father's criticism. He always told me that I could do better, that I had to do more.

He certainly didn't mean to hurt me. Actually, he thought he was nudging me, encouraging me. Yet my level of self-esteem wound up lower than the soles of my feet. I'm sure he didn't realize it. On the contrary, he pushed me precisely because he had faith in my abilities, but at the time I didn't understand. As a child I perceived things differently. My father is still a little anxious and hypochondriacal, but now I try to argue: "Daddy, stop feeling incurably ill. You're almost seventy years old. You used to say you'd be dead before thirty. And then, before forty. And then, before your fifties. But you're still here. Relax!" But I say it with love. I genuinely want him to put his heart at ease. To live a peaceful life.

Zia Marilena kept telling me, "Focus on the positive inside yourself."

"I can't find anything—"

"That's not true! We all have to find and foster the good things about ourselves. You're very perceptive, for starters. And remember, you never have to do anything to gain someone else's approval. You only have to do what makes you right with yourself." It was as if my aunt had taken my hand and shown me the way to go.

5

The hoglet was teeny tiny, with a little belly that was round and a bit cumbersome. His belly stuck out, and his hind legs couldn't reach the ground. When he wanted to move, he dragged himself along with his front legs. I also thought the little hedgehog stumbled too much. I asked myself if this was just a matter of disproportion between his belly and legs, or if a little bit of weakness was to blame? My doubt tinged the image with sadness.

Incessantly anxious, I asked Giulia if it would help to give him vitamins. She wrote me that she would ask her husband, Gérard, who was an expert on hedgehogs in his own right. In the end, we decided to give him a few drops of vitamin B syrup.

How much could the little guy take?

He didn't give up, and his struggles filled me with emotion.

On Wednesday, finally, the puppy formula arrived. It required a preparation that might have been simple for any mother taking care of a newborn, but not me. Awkward and ill-prepared—good thing Giulia was there to explain things and advise me—I alternated between milk, herbal teas, and almond oil, the best a bovine veterinarian could do. However, I was like the proverbial bull in a china shop. And everything seemed too small for my big hands. Starting with the hedgehog.

Giulia wrote in an e-mail:

> Make a tea by brewing fennel seeds in hot water. Let it steep for ten minutes. When the infusion has cooled off, pour a little bit into a mug. Then add the formula powder. Mix it thoroughly, until there are no clumps. When it gets creamy, mix in the rest of the tea, but heat it up first. Mix it again and then your milk is ready.

> To keep it the right temperature while giving it to the hedgehog, it's useful—but not essential—to keep it in a double boiler; i.e., place the cup in a small pot of hot water. Note: The proper ratio is one part formula to two parts fennel tea. To start, though only at first (twenty-four to forty-eight hours), you can dilute it more.

I followed these instructions to the letter. And just before giving the little one his "bottle," I poured a few drops on my wrist to check the temperature. I was on my way to becoming a real Mr. Mom!

The prepared milk could be stored in the refrigerator for

twenty-four hours. But I preferred to make it throughout the day so it would always be fresh. Giulia explained to me that diluting the powder in fennel tea instead of water helps to avoid bloating, which could be very risky for a little hedgehog. But even with this new milk, we didn't change our routine: Every three hours, I weighed the hoglet, prepared his milk, gave it to him with the little syringe, reweighed him, massaged his belly a little, and placed a hot water bottle next to him.

As Giulia had predicted, with proper nutrition, the little one started to thrive. He slept and ate, ate and slept. I watched him, *verklempt*. He'd lie on his side, relaxed. His tiny mouth seemed to form a smile. Usually he crossed his front legs under his chin, the two paws clasped like little hands. It was a sweet image. Or he would lie on his side with front and back legs extended all the way out. He looked like an easel or a bridge.

Often when he woke up, he'd stretch and yawn. It made me laugh. He held his front legs out and at the same time opened his mouth wide, and you could see that little strip of tongue, thin as a rose petal, unfurl. It was so sweet, I was touched.

Every time I held him in my hand, I was astonished at how soft he was. And I loved feeling those little feet flutter in silky steps over my palm. It was like a caress.

One thing that came as no small surprise were the marks I discovered on his abdomen. I looked closer and then I understood: The skin on his belly was so thin you could see through it, like tissue paper. When his stomach was full of milk, a white spot appeared on the left. You could see it clearly—it was like a sack. Further down, on the right, was a dark, almost purple spot. That was his bladder filled with urine. This translucence highlighted for me, once again, a baby hedgehog's extreme fragility.

Anyway, everything seemed to be going perfectly. Then one day, when I came home to feed him, I went over to his box and stopped cold: The white sponge floor of his box was streaked with blood. Red skid marks in all directions. My heart skipped a beat. My eyes stared, fixed as if in a still image. I took the hoglet in my hand. He might be bleeding from the tail, but I couldn't quite tell. Its genitals and anus were also in that area. It wasn't easy to identify the source of the blood loss. Upset, I immediately contacted Giulia. I sent her photos of the hoglet.

She replied fast:

> He's losing blood from his tail. It's irritated because hedgehog urine is so acidic. Gérard says you need to clean the area well and apply an antibiotic cream.

I rushed to treat the hedgehog, and only after having taken care of everything did I notice I had another e-mail from Giulia.

I read it right away, and a smile spread across my face:

> Massimo, I took a closer look at the photos of the hedgehog's "nether regions." Don't worry, the inflammation won't be hard to cure. Oh, and your hoglet . . . it's a girl!

A girl! It made me feel even more protective knowing it was a baby girl. Which isn't true, really—I would have had the same reaction if she had told me it was a boy. It was knowing the gender that was so touching. It wasn't just a "hedgehog" anymore. It was a girl. I had to come up with a name for her.

6

The next day, Greta arrived. We'd known each other for over a year, since we'd traveled to Australia together with a group of mutual friends.

We kept on seeing each other after we returned to Italy, and almost without realizing it, we became a couple. She came over every weekend, and we spent time together.

As soon as she walked in the door, she wanted to see the baby.

"She's grown! Yes, yes. She's a little bigger," she said enthusiastically.

I smiled, unable to hide my satisfaction.

"I can see she sleeps a ton," she continued.

"She eats and sleeps, like all newborns."

"Since she likes to sleep so much, why don't we call her

Ninna, like the lullaby? What do you say, Massimo? Do you like it?"

I liked "Ninna." Meanwhile, in a high-pitched voice, Greta gave the name a try: "Ninna! Ninnaaaa! Are you hungry, Ninna? Are you sleepy, Ninna?"

And so, now my little hedgehog was Ninna.

I wrote to Giulia:

> Ninna is starting to open her eyes!

Indeed, the opening between her eyelids widened day by day. I could see a little bit of her eye. I got the impression, sometimes, that through those tiny openings, the little one was trying to look at me.

Hedgehogs see primarily in black and white, plus a few colors. Not all of them. And, at any rate, their vision isn't very good. But their sense of hearing and smell are very developed. Surely Ninna recognized my scent, because I always handled her without gloves. Soon she would see me. Would she think I was her mama?

Giulia answered my e-mail right away:

> Hoglets open their eyes between two and three weeks of age. That means Ninna is a little older than we thought. Unfortunately, that also means she was, and is, hugely underweight! Check her teeth, because in the third week they start to poke out from the gums. And then you'll have to start weaning. In nature, hoglets that

age would follow their mother out of the nest and learn from her how to procure food by digging in the ground.

I wrote her again:

> In any case, I think Ninna is doing well. She's very lively, she's agile, and sucks on everything she comes upon. And she makes noise: Every once in a while, she shrieks!

Another prompt reply from Giulia:

> When hedgehogs "suckle," it means they're hungry! We need to give her more milk. And soon get started with weaning. For now, try giving Ninna her usual milk in a saucer. At this point, she can learn to eat on her own!

Greta and I put Ninna on the table. She didn't stumble anymore. The formula and vitamins had worked miracles. We brought a spoon full of milk up to her. She dove in. Hedgehogs have very long noses, and their mouths are positioned further back. Her nose beat her mouth to it. She jumped back with a start, blowing out milk left and right. It was hilarious, but it scared me, too. "*Madonnina mia*, she's going to choke! She's choking! The milk went up her nose!" Panic. I sent a text to Giulia, who calmed me down:

> Nothing to fear! Hedgehogs have a part in their nose with a membrane which closes if needed, keeping liquids from getting through.

I felt better. I examined Ninna's little nose: a jewel. It looked like a piece of licorice. Perfect. With those tiny nostrils so clearly defined, it was as if the able hand of a master miniaturist had painted them. Only better. Nothing can top the perfection of nature.

Meanwhile, Ninna kept on snorting out drops. At the same time, with her tongue extended, she licked the milk off her nose.

She learned how to drink by herself pretty quickly. Greta and I watched her, enraptured: Ninna would drink a little, lift her head, swallow, and then go back down to take another sip. A fluid motion—harmonious, continuous.

A wave.

A dance.

At the beginning of the next week, still following Giulia's instructions to the letter, I bought some freeze-dried meat for kittens.

I read and reread her latest e-mail:

> Massimo, by now I know you well and can pre-empt you.
> :) When you give Ninna this new food, don't have a heart
> attack!!! Let me warn you: You'll see the hoglet start to
> tremble and then . . . it will spit up. RELAX! She might
> twist around and seem all contorted, but don't freak out!
> It's normal for a hedgehog to do that when it encounters
> a totally new flavor. It's called self-anointing.

Self-anointing? I was amazed and curious. I supplemented the usual formula with the tip of a teaspoon's worth of meat powder. I mixed it together and put the concoction on a plate. I placed it in front of Ninna. And the show began.

Ninna tasted it. Right away her eyes gaped open, and she produced a kaleidoscope of grimaces that wrinkled her whole muzzle. You could die laughing! She seemed on the point of saying, "What the heck is this stuff you're making me eat now?" Then she panted a little and started mixing the food with her saliva. A little foam appeared on the sides of her mouth—thank goodness Giulia had warned me, otherwise I really would have had a coronary—and then the little thing began to contort. She bent her neck and arched her body. She thus tried to reach all along her back and spread the foam over her spines. But, clumsy like all pups, she wobbled left and right and kept tipping over, winding up on her back with her legs pedaling in the air.

Hedgehogs begin the strange practice of self-anointing when they're babies and continue as adults. No one knows for sure the reason for this behavior. It may be to camouflage their scent. Or, since over time it produces a notable stench, maybe it's a way of making a "do-it-yourself" repellant. Who knows.

Little by little, I began to increase the amount of meat powder and reduce the quantity of milk. Weaning would end when she was forty days old. At that point, I wouldn't give her milk anymore, so as not to risk a dangerous intolerance. Ninna continued to grow and became, if possible, even more lovely. Whereas I—after so many sleepless nights and days spent racing between her and my job—was physically wrecked. Thinner, with dark circles under my eyes, I yearned for a whole night of uninterrupted sleep. It seemed like a mirage.

It was Friday night again. Greta came over. She hugged me and then rushed over to Ninna.

"Can I pick her up?" she asked me.

"I'd rather you didn't. You might drop her."

But as if I hadn't said anything, she'd already picked her up, lifted her to her face, and nuzzled her gently against her cheek. Yes, I admit, I was a little possessive. However, I really was afraid she could fall. I plucked Ninna out of her hands and put her back in her box. I had to leave for an important appointment, but I felt uneasy. I told Greta not to pick her up again, to let her rest, and we would feed her when I got back.

I returned a little later than expected. The house was silent, as if no one were home. I quickly headed to Ninna. The box was empty. Worry came out of my pores. I ran nervously from room to room, searching for Greta. I found her in the bedroom. She was lying on the bed, two pillows under her head, the sheet up to her chin. I didn't even say hello. Instead I jumped on her. "Where's Ninna?" My angry voice met her serene gaze. With enigmatic flourish, putting her index finger to her lips, she whispered, "Shh!" She folded the sheet down. Ninna was curled up on her chest asleep, her tiny mouth bent in its usual smile.

Greta protected her with a hand. I stood there breathless. An unforgettable image. Beautiful as a painting. She loved cuddling that little creature.

"Do you realize that if you had fallen asleep you could have crushed her?" I said, but all my anxiety and irritation had melted.

7

Zio Osvaldo. Long, black hair and piercing green eyes. The same green as the forest in June, when the leaves are their brightest and the sun highlights their color, warming them with flashes of golden light. When I was a kid, he was a young man. My big brother—uncle. Partner in play and adventure. Together we would always search for animals to rescue. Once it was a little bird that fell from its nest. Another time a butterfly with a crushed wing. We built little homes for them. We caught insects for baby birds. We brought bouquets of flowers to butterflies.

We created a little pond by digging a suitable hole in a field. We put water in it and—*ecco!*—a pond. Zio Osvaldo took me fishing nearby. We caught fish with a net, often gorgeous carp with hints of red. They were supposed to be for lunch or dinner, but we granted some a pardon, placing them in the little artificial pond. I topped off the water several times a week, drawing it from a stream that ran near my grandparents' house. One day, a little upstream, a woman had done some laundry. I hadn't noticed that the water I was adding to the pond was contaminated with her soap. Not until the fish began gasping at the surface. Desperate, I ran to find my uncle. I remember the anguish. And the guilt. He helped me move the fish to safety in a vat with clear water. We then took all the soapy liquid from the pond and replaced it with clean water—a long and tiring task. Afterward, however, the carp and other little fish could once again splash around in their home.

One time Zio Osvaldo and I found two jays. The circumstances of this discovery are lost in a fog of shapeless memories. I only remember they were chicks. We put them in a big cage and took very good care of them. We called them Cheep and Chop. I was fascinated by the blue-and-white designs on their wings, by their liveliness and their alert eyes, but even more so by their imitations. They were able to reproduce the calls of other birds and our own childish laughter. And they could talk. They repeated certain words—for example, our names.

It was incredible!

We fed Cheep and Chop acorns, nuts, insects, and bits of meat.

I gave all my animals a name, even some of the chickens my Nonna Caterina raised.

I remember one in particular: I called it Limpie. It was a chick that could barely stand on its feet. They were twisted, maybe even a little deformed.

"I think Limpie is sick. Can I take care of him? Can I keep him?" I pestered my grandmother.

"Come on, Mama. Give it to Massimo," Zio Osvaldo said in support. "Want to bet he'll be able to cure it?"

When we successfully wrangled her into agreeing, I started bringing the young chicken out into the sun. Every day. I was sure it was good for him. In the evening, I put him near the wood-burning stove. I fed him and made sure he always had fresh, clean water. I talked to him. I petted him exceedingly. I was probably causing him stress.

Nevertheless, my heart and my child's remedies performed a miracle, or so it seemed. Limpie's legs, little by little, grew stronger. And then they straightened up. He started to support himself better, then to walk a few steps, then to take short runs. Cured! Perhaps the chick suffered from some type of rickets that had gone away. Who knows, maybe the exposure to the sun really had made him better.

"It started to run because it couldn't stand your coddling

anymore," my uncle joked, hugging me and lifting me up. And we both started laughing like crazy.

"Grandma, promise me we'll never eat Limpie!" I begged her one day. That was the unavoidable fate of animals raised on the farm. She smiled and kissed my forehead. To seal the promise.

I also went searching for slugs with my uncle. Snails, actually. He told me to put on my boots, and we grabbed a pair of buckets and headed out. We would go just as it was about to stop raining. We caught tons of them. Back home, the buckets were delivered to Grandma. But secretly, I'd free handfuls of them. I was afraid Zio Osvaldo might notice, but I knew he'd never rat me out. Or get mad at me.

Sometimes he and I would lie in wait near a bird's nest. We kept still and silent and watched the parents feed their children. Transfixed, we didn't move a muscle so as not to disturb them.

I also liked watching cows graze. To me they exuded such serenity. Freedom. An image that still warms my heart today. It's peace. It's nature in harmony.

I had three loves as a boy: drawing, stargazing, and helping animals. I didn't choose art or astronomy. I decided to attend veterinary school.

I dreamed of traveling and being an animal doctor, in Africa perhaps, in contact with the wild.

Or I could focus on bovines and work in the open air, out in the country.

Zio Osvaldo's presence during my childhood fostered my love of animals and nature.

My big brother-uncle passed away when he was still young. I imagine Zio Osvaldo in a paradise that befits him. I can see him, long hair tousled by the wind, with his forest-colored eyes, with warblers, sparrows, and jays flying around him and landing on his shoulders. The jays chat with him and echo his laughter.

8

Ninna was changing.

As the days passed, fur began to grow all over her body, fur that spread out more or less uniformly. First it emerged over her muzzle, the sides of her nose. It formed like a bunch of tiny buttons that gradually expanded. In some parts, for a very short while, her little body looked like a map. But soon, like a field where the grass grows before your eyes, she was completely covered in a thick carpet. The dark quills on her back became more noticeable. Her nose, ears, and nails grew. She lost her babyish features and took on the appearance of an adult. That was it—she looked just like an adult hedgehog, but in miniature.

I decided that the box she was living in was too small. Between the liner, food plate, water bowl, and Ninna, there

wasn't much room left. I bought a cage—a rabbit hutch, actually—three by five feet, the largest I could find. I set it all up,
covering the bottom with layers of newspaper. It seemed to fit
my hedgie perfectly. She pattered back and forth, and once she
got tired, she went under the little blanket I'd set in the corner.

She was adorable with her dish of food. She'd crouch all the
way down and slide her nose under it. Then she'd pitch it up,
and it would drop down with a thump. After several tries, she
achieved her goal: both plate and food upside down. Then she
looked satisfied.

Giulia wrote me:

> Ninna needs a house now. Use a cardboard box. A
> shoebox would work fine. On one side, cut an opening
> Ninna can go in and out of when she wants. You should
> put strips of paper in the house. You can use cut-up
> newspapers or parchment paper. Hedgehogs like to
> have hay. Do you think you could get some? If you put
> some of these things next to the house as well, Ninna
> will take them herself and finish building her nest as she
> likes!

I got to work right away and made a house out of cardboard
a little smaller than a shoebox, but perfect for a hedgehog of
Ninna's size. As soon as it was finished, I put it in the cage.
Ninna walked over to it, curious but wary. She sniffed at it. She
gave the walls a little lick. Then a more insistent lick, and then
another.

After her house tasting, she decided to spend some time self-anointing, since the house's flavor was new to her. Have completed this "task," she stuck her head through the door, lifted the house, and slid inside. A few seconds later, she came back out. She started going in and out repeatedly, carefully exploring its interior and exterior, engrossed. When I set some hay and paper strips next to the opening, she took them in her mouth and, little by little, took them inside the box. Now I was sure she liked the house.

She slept peacefully in it, but when she heard a noise, she'd poke out. Sometimes just her nose, if she thought a sniff was enough to analyze the surroundings. It was like she always wanted to be aware of everything going on around her.

I liked when Ninna looked at me. She had sparkling, curious eyes. She turned her little head up toward me, and I would talk to her. She listened to my voice. Sometimes, in a wave of enthusiasm, I would sing her a song or a lullaby. I also liked it when she crawled onto my hands, my fingers. She smelled me meticulously. Sometimes she would try to squeeze into the sleeve of my shirt or sweater. In any case, we had a good rapport, even if we communicated in different ways.

I began offering her different kinds of meat, to vary her diet. I also added fresh fruit. I wanted to enrich the menu with lots of vegetables, but Giulia wrote me:

> No, that's not necessary. Hedgehogs aren't
> vegetarians!!!

When I placed the food bowl in her cage, Ninna didn't come out of her house. She took it with her. You know how snails do? Like that. She went over to the bowl with her house on top of her. Only her muzzle appeared through the door. The rest of her body remained inside. As she ate, the house moved up and down with her. She hadn't lost her obsession with flipping her dish, but now she preferred to do it with her water bowl. After the usual *thump thump thump*, a pool spread over the newspaper lining the bottom of the cage.

I looked around and spotted an old ashtray. It was heavy crystal. The perfect bowl! And indeed, the thumping stopped.

Giulia explained:

> Now Ninna needs a meal in the late afternoon and
> another one at night. You might give her a little
> something to eat first thing in the morning, too. Put her
> cage in a room with a window or two, so the little one
> will be exposed to the natural rhythms of night and day,
> dark and light. Oh, and I almost forgot: During the day,
> she should sleep, like all hedgehogs! One last thing:
> Does Ninna bite?

I thought about that last question. I typed my reply:

> Well, Ninna gnaws and bites at everything. But not
> people, definit—

I didn't even finish before I was surprised by a loud "ow!" shouted from the next room, where Ninna was. I got there in a nanosecond. "Greta, what happened?"

"Nothing!" she replied, holding her right hand behind her back and trying to look nonchalant.

"Did Ninna bite you?"

"No, no."

"Let me see," I told her. The tip of her index finger was a little red.

It had happened. But it wasn't hard. Just a nibble. Maybe Ninna was irritated, or perhaps she'd mistaken Greta's finger for something she could eat. Either way, the little creature observed the scene with some interest, without any sense of guilt. But the timing of Giulia's question was incredible! I advised Greta to be especially careful with Ninna and returned to the e-mail I'd left unfinished. I erased:

> But not people, definit—

and wrote:

> Not me, ever. However, my girlfriend experienced her teeth just now :(.

Greta came up to me right after that, her left hand supporting her right. The finger in question was pointed and held apart from the others. I felt bad, but it was really no big deal.

"So are we going to the beach tomorrow?" she asked me in

a little voice, like a victim. Crap! We had planned the trip awhile ago, and I had forgotten all about it. But how could I resist the young martyr Greta? My two dogs would be easy to farm out. "But what will we do with Ninna?" I asked back.

9

We decided on a quick trip to the sea. We'd leave the next morning—Saturday—and come back late Sunday afternoon. And we'd take Ninna along. I certainly couldn't have left her at home: Who would take care of her? I packed a bag with the bare necessities: two random shirts, a pair of shorts, flip-flops, a toothbrush, etc. I was done in five minutes. Greta's bag was already packed. So we started getting Ninna ready. What did I need to bring for her? Well . . . her cage, of course, newspaper for the bottom, her cardboard house, her water and food bowls, her blanket, a towel, everything for preparing her meals, her hay, a roll of paper towels, etc.

I found myself thinking how crazy it was that such a small being needed so much stuff! After an hour and a half, her bags were ready. Another thought popped into my head: Before meeting Ninna, it definitely would have taken me an hour and a half to pack my bags.

It made me laugh a little.

It took me longer to load the car because I wanted Ninna to be comfortable and safe in her cage. I tried several arrangements before getting it right.

Finally, we were ready. But it had come time to feed the little one. What could we do? Feeding her right before we left meant she might throw up. But I didn't have the heart to let her go hungry. I didn't want that or to risk making her weak. I decided on a light meal, followed by a short rest so she could digest.

It was late by the time we managed to get out the door. I was behind the wheel, Greta beside me, Ninna behind. I drove slowly so as not to upset the little one too much. But she was stressed. She hid under her blanket, then she'd pop out in a corner and start pacing around her cage. Then she'd try to climb up the walls before going back under her blanket, only to come out almost immediately and start the whole dance over again. She was definitely disturbed. Nervous, I'd say. I felt guilty for having put her in this situation. When the road was all twists and turns, it was even worse because Ninna was tossed left and right. We stopped at least ten times, to let her calm down.

"You think she'd relax if I held her?" Greta asked at a certain point.

"It's not ideal, you know. If I had to brake suddenly, she might fall. But I am going pretty slow . . . All right, let's try," I said.

So Greta took Ninna, set her on her knees, and covered her with the blanket, to make her feel more secure. But the little hedgehog was uncontrollable. You could see all her movements under the little cover, which bounced and fluttered constantly. Her nose would pop out from one side and then the other, in rapid succession.

"Take away the cover. Maybe it's bothering her," I suggested. But that didn't work.

"Maybe she wants to look out the window," Greta said laughing, but it was a laugh dotted with stress.

And we were only halfway there.

A few miles farther, a police patrol signaled for us to pull over. One of the two officers came up to the window. "License and registration." I handed them over. He took his time to run the check. So I asked him, "Everything okay?"

"Yeah, yeah," he replied. But at the same time, waving my documents in his hands, he started examining the car.

"Your tires are bald. I have to write you up," he declared. I remembered I had an appointment that coming Monday at the tire store, but I didn't tell him that. There was little chance he'd believe me and not give me a ticket.

"Today is really a bad day," I thought, looking down at the steering wheel.

"What's that?" the policeman asked, pointing at Ninna. He'd just noticed her.

"It's a baby hedgehog," I answered.

"Come get a look at this," he said to the other officer, who was waiting nearby, leaning against his motorcycle.

Both of them, their heads craning through the window, looked at Ninna in awe.

"How cute! Is it a boy or a girl?" the first policeman asked.

"How old is it?" the other chimed in.

I told them the whole story as they listened intently, even a bit fascinated. Meanwhile, Ninna relaxed.

In the end, they decided not to give me a ticket.

"You're a good vet. But change those tires as soon as possible," the first officer said. Then, perhaps to hide his emotion, he said good-bye with a little joke: "Take it easy. Drive carefully. You've got the whole family in the car!" He laughed, and we laughed along with him.

We finally made it to the sea, but not without more—many more—stops so Ninna could rest. Moreover, she vomited at some point, hurling my sense of guilt through the roof.

Once we found the apartment where we were staying—which belonged to some friends—we unloaded Ninna and her cage. We set her up in a corner of the spacious kitchen, then took care of the rest. And Greta and I finally went to the beach. But my mind constantly drifted to the little creature who was now in an unfamiliar house. I wasn't sure she felt comfortable.

Also, I would have liked to show her the sea. But that wasn't possible. Too much sun, too many people.

However.

I was formulating a plan. After a nice dinner and a romantic walk, Greta went to bed. Not me. I had to wait for Ninna's feeding time. When I was sure my girlfriend was asleep, I put my plan into motion. I grabbed a hat I always kept in the car, put Ninna inside it, and tiptoed out of the apartment. I went to the pier and sat down where the jetty disappeared into the cliffs. It was late, and there weren't many people around. Just a couple of fishermen farther away. My little Ninna's face popped out from the hat. Her quick, shining eyes looked around. Her nose sniffed the air in search of new stories. It was a starry night.

"Ninna, this is the sea. Without me, you never would have seen it," I whispered to her. We stayed there a long time, lulled by the music of the waves and enveloped in the salty air. I crept back in as quietly as I'd left. I didn't want Greta to hear me. She already knew I was a little crazy, but I didn't want her to start really believing it.

The next day, in the afternoon, we returned home. Trip over. But I was happy because Ninna had seen the sea. And I'd learned something: Hedgehogs can get carsick and can help you get out of tickets. I hadn't realized, though, that I was humanizing Ninna too much. I had fallen into thinking of her as a baby. My baby. But that wasn't good.

10

loved watching Ninna and found every little thing she did so sweet. Often when I got back from work, I'd take her out of her cage and let her roam around the house a bit. At first, she was wary, but in no time she got used to it. She would patter around everywhere. "Ninna, Ninnaaa," I called, and many times, she would come running. Not always, though. If she was occupied with something she deemed more interesting, I came in second.

I was getting very attached to her. And to think that when I was little, I'd promised myself not to let other animals into my heart.

Nero was a wound that had left me with a big scar, a mark on my soul. I was 6 or so when some friends of my father's gave him to us. The puppy was chubby, strong, and beautiful. All black, except for the spots on his nose. Surely his family tree included various breeds, but in him the German shepherd was clearly predominant. I remember our first night with him. We closed him in the kitchen, but I could hear his yelping all the way in my room. So I quietly slid out of bed, went to him, and comforted him, petting him for a long time. Without a sound, I brought him to bed with me. Nero calmed down, and we slept side by side. And we did so every night thereafter. When I got home from school, he would greet me excitedly. For us both, it was a joy.

But the puppy grew up and got bored being by himself all day. In the house from eight to five, he got into all kinds of trouble. Finally my parents decided—for everybody's good, including Nero's—to leave him with my grandparents. He'd have more space to run and play and more company. Zio Osvaldo would take care of him. For me, it was devastating to be separated from my dog, even though my parents would take me to visit him after work every few days. And I got to enjoy him during school holidays. Then, we were inseparable.

One day, he and I were wandering around in the fields. We had gone out farther than normal. I was on my bike, and he happily followed behind. We passed by a farm, and I saw a boy, older than me, with a big, ferocious-looking dog. I was afraid. I could sense something dramatic was about to happen, something brutal. And then, the boy sicced his dog on us. Nero and I had nowhere to go. We couldn't get away. They were too close. That dog would be on us in a matter of seconds.

I was frozen. Nero—all the fur on his body standing on end—didn't back down.

Like darts, the two heaved themselves at each other. Jaws open, bright-white fangs bared. After a violent tussle, the other dog started to back away and retreat. Nero had won the battle. He came back to me, his eyes still on fire. There was a streak of blood under his right ear, but nothing serious. We dashed out of there.

My dog had protected me. He'd saved me. I always felt safe with him.

A few years later, Nero got run over by a truck while I was at school. When they told me, I was heartbroken. I cried all the tears a little boy has in him. That was when I swore I would never get attached to an animal again. I wouldn't let my heart get broken like that again.

Never again! And so it was.

That is, until I met Lilly.

After I graduated from college, my parents split up, but—contrary to my childish fears—I didn't lose them when they got divorced. They were happier that way, as was I. Sometimes people would abandon dogs near my mother's house. Word had spread that she would take care of them. Sometimes there were even pregnant females, so there would be puppies later on, too.

One day a few years ago, my mother called me and said, "Massimo, I'm really worried about this puppy. I don't know what happened, but one of her paws is hurting her. Actually, she won't even put her weight on it. You have to come and have a look as soon as you can." I rushed over. The little thing—a red Volpino, female, five or six months old—had a fractured paw. I took her to Remo, a colleague of mine who specialized in small animal orthopedics. He confirmed my diagnosis and told me he'd operate a few days later. I kept the puppy until the surgery, which I assisted, and it all went fine. In order to oversee her recovery, I took the puppy to my place.

"Call her Lilly. She looks like a Lilly!" a neighbor suggested one day. So Lilly it was.

One month after the operation, she needed another, to remove the pin that had been inserted to mend the fracture. I set up a time with Remo and took her over. Without realizing it, I'd grown attached to that little puppy—to the extent that the second surgery seemed to drag on forever, even though it was actually much faster and simpler than the first. What anxiety I had! I was definitely emotionally involved.

When the operation was finished, the puppy lay on her side with an IV still in. Her eyes were closed. I went over, bent down to her, and whispered, "Lilly . . . Lillyyy . . ." The only response was the continuous *thump, thump, thump, thump* of her tail hitting the steel post-operation table. She couldn't reply, but she wagged her tail at the sound of my voice. I was touched. With that little tail, she stole my heart for good.

But I swore to myself, just her! No one else!

A few months later, my mother called me about Jack, a

puppy who'd had a bout of diarrhea. I brought him home to take care of him. Lilly was jealous, but they quickly became fast friends. And Jack was so lovable and affectionate! Once he recovered, he kept me company while I built a stone wall in the yard. Constantly by my side, he started playing with the stones I was using. He still has an obsession with them to this day. I think he's the only dog in the world who spends time transporting stones. If there's a rock around, he feels obligated to take it in his front paws and drag it backward from one spot to another. He's a strong dog; he'll even pick up big stones, leaving furrows in the grass.

When I realized I was attached to him too, I promised myself again: just Jack and Lilly! No one else!

As I watched Ninna scampering through the kitchen, I found myself thinking, "Okay, okay! Just Lilly, Jack, and Ninna!" What a disaster! But that's just how I am.

11

I only let Ninna roam free through the house under my direct supervision. Left to her own devices, she could start chewing on an electric cord or eat something that would harm her. Or get herself into some sort of trouble. There were too many dangers.

But I loved hearing her walk around! It made me happy. And she seemed cheerful and playful. When I put her back in her cage, she sent me clear signals of discontent. She couldn't stand being confined anymore. She'd pace back and forth without stopping, visibly aggravated. Especially at night. I brought her cage into my room, thinking that being able to hear me might calm her down.

It didn't work. I woke up a hundred times and always found her clinging to the walls of her prison, with her little nose pok-

A HANDFUL of HAPPINESS

ing out from the netting, looking at me, her eyes piercing. She seemed like she wanted to ask me for something.

Before, I didn't sleep because I had to feed her; now, I couldn't sleep because she was making a horrible racket. I was getting burned out. For my own survival, I moved the cage back into the other room. But this didn't eliminate the problem of Ninna's restlessness.

And I couldn't stand her being unhappy.

I shared my new problem with Giulia. She wrote back quickly:

> Ninna weighs over three hundred grams now. You can put her in a pen outside. Little by little, she will readjust to her natural habitat. She'll be happier. You'll see, she'll even learn how to hunt.

I chose a suitable place in the yard and fenced it off. I put Ninna there often. She frolicked around, pleased with this half-freedom. But I, anxious as always, didn't let her out of my sight.

Meanwhile, a trip I'd had planned for a long time—since January, to be precise—was approaching. Departure was scheduled for mid-August.

It wasn't just any vacation, it was my life dream.

It was a trip through Africa with three of my best friends: Enrico, a veterinarian and a mentor of mine; Matteo, another veterinarian and lifelong friend; and Dario, the only non-vet, but a friend and an all-around good guy. It was an organized tour. There would be another ten or eleven people, plus the guide and drivers. We would arrive in Namibia, cross the Kalahari Desert to Botswana, and then travel to various national parks, ending at Victoria Falls.

I was torn between two emotions: a boundless desire to take this trip and a bottomless sorrow to leave Ninna.

If I were to go, who would watch her? This was a real problem. It wasn't a trip to the seashore. I couldn't just bring her along. I talked to my mother and my cousin Francesco. He's Zio Osvaldo's only son. He takes after him, too. The same big heart. The same love of animals and nature. Francesco told me right away, "Massimo, you go, and rest assured, I can take care of Ninna. Trust me!"

"And I'm here! I can take care of her, too," my mother chimed in enthusiastically.

Everybody loves Ninna!

I trusted both of them, completely.

Francesco and I would build a pen in my mother's yard. Every night they'd put Ninna inside it for a few hours. I didn't want her there all night. I was afraid of a hostile visit from some nocturnal predator. The rest of the time, she'd stay in her cage. I gave them all her feeding instructions and concluded, of course, with several other pieces of advice. They both listened carefully. It truly was the ideal solution. Plus, Francesco lived right across from my mother, which would make it easy for him to come and go.

We built Ninna's pen under a cherry tree. The dense foliage would supply the necessary shade. We made a rectangle with corrugated plastic sheets and planted it four inches into the ground. That way, if Ninna decided to dig a tunnel out—hedgehogs dig!—she'd be blocked. For good measure, we placed stones all around the perimeter for extra safety. When it was finished, the pen was ten by thirteen feet and one and a half feet tall. Inside, we placed Ninna's new house on a brick base: a wooden house that used to be a box of fine wine. I had made a hole on one side for the door and gave it a reinforced roof, insulated with nylon. Then, with Francesco's help, I placed an awning over part of the pen right over the house. This way, even if there was an unexpected storm, Ninna could take shelter.

The eve of my departure arrived. I had everything prepared but was still wavering. It was a very expensive trip, and I'd already paid the full amount in advance. If it were possible to get my money back, maybe I could back out . . .

That night, I loaded Ninna and all her bags in the car. Then I put Lilly and Jack in and left for my mother's. She and Francesco were expecting me. The two dogs were used to staying there when I went on vacation or had to go away for a few days. They happily leapt to greet both her and my cousin and then went off in search of their favorite spots, just to make sure everything was the same since the last time they'd been there. For Ninna, however, it was all new.

I checked every inch of the pen one more time. And I went through everything Mama and Francesco had to do for Ninna once again. Then I finally left my "kids" in their good hands, and only after endless farewells did I return to my place.

Coming home without Lilly and Jack's cheerful welcome or Ninna's scampering left and right made me feel alone. A shiver ran down my spine. There was too much silence. It was full, round—deafening. The house seemed needlessly large. And above all, empty. I found myself thinking, as I tossed and turned in bed, how selfish I was: I'd put a vacation before my two dogs and hedgehog. They would have been calmer at home and maybe even safer. I was worried about Ninna. How would she react to not seeing me? And being handled by people she didn't know? What if she fell? Or ran away? Tormented, all my worries kept my eyes wide open. I drifted off just when the light of dawn began to take over the dark. By then it was just a couple of hours before I had to leave for the airport. One thing was certain: Since I'd met Ninna, for one reason or another, I'd never had a single night of peaceful sleep.

12

I recall every moment of Africa, starting with the sky I found before my eyes as I stepped off the plane. It was a resplendent blue, complete and unbroken. Nary a cloud. Nary anything. I was instantly enveloped by the crisp air, which I eagerly welcomed. It, too, seemed to shine.

I knew that ancient land from my school textbooks, from a thousand television documentaries, yet it astonished me. Intoxicated my senses with wonder.

Broken up into groups, we traveled by car: a caravan of four-by-fours, one behind the other in single file, loaded with everything from tents to food. The roads were wide, long, straight; everything around us flat and endless. Red sand. Green shrubs dotted here and there. Black silhouettes of umbrella-shaped trees. I remember every sunrise and every sunset. The sky would burst into flame and turn the color of fire, with different shades each time. At the Okavango River delta—which doesn't empty into the sea but fades into the desert—we left the cars behind and canoed through the waterways surrounded by reeds and islets. After that, we traveled by car again to the Zimbabwe border. We were in total contact with nature, full immersion. Hippos, elephants, lions, giraffes, wildebeests, baboons, hyenas, crocodiles. And many others. And too many species of birds to name. And a leopard. Yes, just one. They're not easy to spot. My eyes couldn't contain it all. Even the nighttime stars were too much. A mythical journey. More than that: magical.

Every night we found a suitable place to stop, parked the cars in a circle, and pitched the tents in between. Then we set up a row of picnic tables. We all ate together, commenting on our experiences that day.

But that's not all.

On the first night, my fellow adventurers saw me walking all around the campsite trying to find a phone signal. When I wandered a little too far, the guide quickly advised me to be careful because it was extremely dangerous. I told him that I absolutely had to call my mother. As soon as I got back, a few people in the group teased me, saying: "Gotta call your mommy, do you now?" Someone else took the bait: "You miss your mom. What a mama's boy!" More echoed, while others tittered.

"No no, I'm just worried about Ninna and need to check in," I explained.

"Ninna?" three or four asked in unison.

And so it was that every night—in Africa!—I found myself talking about my little hedgehog, how I'd met her, how I'd nursed her, how I'd taken care of her. A miniseries. Yes, we talked about lions and vultures, warthogs and gazelles . . . and Ninna . . . till late, when it was time for bed.

It became a ritual. I searched for a spot where I got cellular service and called my mother.

We kept it short: "Hi, Mama, how are you?"

"Fine. You?"

"Fine. How's Ninna?"

"Good."

"Okay. Talk to you tomorrow."

Then I'd go back to the dinner table, and everyone would ask, "How's Ninna?"

Later, as our conversations died down, the voices of the night became clearer. The darkness filled with rustles, cries, crackles, calls. One night we were startled by a lion's powerful roar. A big lion, close by. It had filled the air enough to rattle our spirits. We all fell silent, our eyes jumping around, uncertain. Full of wonder. And a sort of respect. Some had a barely concealed look of fear. The guide told us that it could be dangerous, we should retire to our tents. There, we would be safe. So that's what we did.

That night, for some of us, it was harder to sleep. I was sharing a tent with Enrico. I woke him up around three: "Enrico, listen . . . the roaring is further away now." In fact, it was deeper, but muffled. Muted, yet still robust. We listened.

"Yeah, he's going away."

Then we burst out laughing. It wasn't actually the voice of the king of the jungle, but one of our travel companions with the most incredible snore I'd ever heard. I'm sure his thunderous, rhythmic purr—or roar—kept all the animals of the savannah at a respectful distance every night.

Near the end of the trip, we went to Victoria Falls. But I couldn't enjoy that exceptional sight. The indisputable beauty of that cascade of water, its impetuous force, deafening rumble, countless rainbows, and clouds of mist reached my heart but couldn't capture it. I was too worried. I hadn't managed to get in touch with my mother for three days. The phone just kept ringing. I was afraid something had happened.

Maybe she wasn't picking up to avoid giving me bad news about Ninna. My anxiety became more evident with every passing hour.

Inevitably, it came time to return home. I got off the plane, and we all piled into the bus for the terminal. I sat down in the back, and the first thing I did was take my phone and shakily type in my mother's number. Finally she answered.

"Mama, I've been calling for days! Are you okay? What happened?" I yelled, agitated.

"Yes. Well, something did happen . . ." she said in a soft voice.

"What is it? What happened?" I repeated, worked up.

"I have some bad news," she went on, her voice trembling.

"Tell me, Mama, you're stressing me out! Did Ninna die?" I shouted again, with all the breath in my lungs and all my desperation.

In the bus, an eerie silence fell. You couldn't hear a fly. One by one, my travel mates turned to look at me, frozen.

"Did Ninna die?" I thundered again, about to burst into tears.

On the other end, a silence bristling with tension.

A soft murmur spread through the group.

"Ninna's dead . . ."

"Ninna's dead . . ."

Funereal looks.

Everyone had come to love the little hedgehog I'd told them all about.

I was in agony, my eyes bulging, my mouth bone-dry.

My mother continued: "It happened so fast . . ."

"Mama, WHAT HAPPENED?"

"I fell and . . . I fractured my wrist."

"*Madonnina mia!* That's it? You fractured your wrist? Thank goodness!"

My onlookers exchanged radiant smiles and several said, "No, it's nothing. Everything's okay! Ninna's alive! Massimo's mother just broke her wrist!"

The packed bus heaved a sigh of relief.

"What do you mean, 'That's it'?" she replied in a whisper.

"Sorry, sorry, Mama, I'm sorry. I was just afraid that . . . I mean . . . you know, a wrist can heal. I love you. I'll be there soon," I replied, sheepishly remorseful but calm.

13

My mother was waiting for me at the door. I went to greet her with open arms, but Lilly and Jack came between us. With nonstop jumps, twists, barks, and whimpers. Lilly rolled over on the ground, belly up. Then she turned and euphorically nuzzled my legs. The cycle went on. Only after several rounds of ebullient greetings did the two dogs calm down, and finally I embraced my mother. Then Francesco appeared. More hugs.

"So, Ninna?" I asked them both.

Ninna had already sensed my presence. Maybe she recognized my voice or my scent. She wasn't in her cardboard house, but was clinging to the side of the cage. Her little eyes were fixed on me as she sniffed excitedly.

"Ninna, Ninnaaa," I called, and it was like she wanted to break through those bars at all costs.

"Let me get her for you," Francesco said, reaching out for her to climb onto his open hand. He passed her to me. I took her and brought her up to my face. Ninna started licking me all over. She paused a moment only to turn in my hands, then she resumed lapping at me uncontrollably. At my fingers, too. She was beyond excited. She seemed happy. So was I.

"When you picked Ninna up, she felt safe. She didn't try to turn over or ball up," I said to Francesco as soon as the hoglet had begun to calm down.

"Yes, we made friends. She trusts me."

"She's grown so much! In these two weeks, you really took good care of her."

"It was easy. She's charming."

I looked at him, smiling. I knew what he meant. He was just like Zio Osvaldo. Physically, there was little resemblance, though he's a handsome young man—in a different way, but also attractive. Blond with clear blue eyes. And a muscular body that girls went crazy over.

Francesco has a little zoo at his house: ponies, dogs, cats, parakeets. A little of everything. And he looks after them with love and attention. He's a good man. Like his father was.

At that moment, as we were talking about Ninna, it occurred to me (as it had many times before) that our relationship was like mine and Zio Osvaldo's. Only now the roles were reversed: I felt like the big brother. And Francesco was like the little brother.

My mother shouted from the kitchen, "Massimo, are you staying to eat?"

"Yes, yes," I replied. Then I turned to Francesco. "Stay too, please. We have so much to catch up on." He nodded, smiling, then yelled to my mother, "Zia Franca, set another place at the table. I'm staying, too."

I was still there the next day. I realized that my mother was having a hard time with her fractured wrist, and I wanted to help her out. Plus, I wanted to spend some time with her. And Francesco, too. I thought I'd stay a week at most. But it ended up being much longer. My mother and my cousin transmitted familial warmth. I was happy there.

I started handling the grocery shopping, the dishes, and things of that sort. My mother prepared all her special recipes. She was content.

I always got back from work in the late afternoon, and Francesco would arrive soon after. We'd take long walks through the fields and nearby woods. We'd talk about this and that: animals, nature, women, work, the future.

We shared our personal lives and gave each other advice. I told him about my bitterness when my ex-wife and I got divorced. That mutual listening was important. It led us to new reflections and perhaps in a way helped me to get rid of some of my sorrows and fears.

On one of those evenings, I told him about an idea that had been buzzing around in my head. "You know what I'd really like to do? I'd like to start a center to help hedgehogs in trouble. Ninna has inspired me. That little creature I met by chance has really changed something inside me."

"A hedgehog center? That's pretty unusual."

"Yes, a center equipped to rescue as many as possible . . ." I trailed off, leaving room for my imagination.

I went on: "Ninna has heightened my desire to help the smallest, the most forgotten. Precisely because no one hardly ever thinks of them. Whereas every creature, even the tiniest, is precious. First and foremost, it's a life. But it's also an important part of our planet, a piece without which the puzzle is incomplete, an indispensable element of the harmony of the whole."

We both fell silent to unravel our thoughts. For several minutes.

"And I must be here to do something with this life of mine, right?" I continued, not expecting a response.

"Who knows, maybe nothing happens purely by chance. Maybe you were meant to meet Ninna. To find this path, to make your own way," Francesco said.

"I'll build some pens at my house. There's room. It's so big! And I'll put all the needy hedgehogs there."

"I'll help, too, Massimo."
I knew I could count on him.

The next day, I wrote to Giulia about my project, but she threw water on the flames of my enthusiasm. She replied:

> It's not that easy. To house hedgehogs, you need permits, official permits. It might be easier for you to help at a center that's already approved and active.

As always, she was right. The law states that if you find a hedgehog, you're supposed to take it to a wild animal rescue center. Or you can leave it with a veterinarian. I'm a vet, so then it's fine, right? No, even a veterinarian can only keep a hedgehog, or any other wild animal, for the amount of time necessary to provide care. And then you're supposed to take it to a center where the staff will see to its shelter, for varying lengths of time depending on the case, before releasing it back into nature.

I called the director of the Wildlife Recovery Center in Cuneo, introduced myself, and offered to help them with any hedgehogs they had. He was enthusiastic about me joining their group. However, I didn't start volunteering right away. This newly born idea of mine needed time to grow. I nursed it and thought about how to make it happen. I felt like someone who goes after his dreams. And I liked it.

The days unfolded one after another and still I hadn't gone back home.

"Stay a little longer," my mother said. And I didn't know how to—nor did I want to—tell her no. I wanted to linger in the warmth and closeness we'd developed during that time.

Perfect moments.

One morning, I was having a quick breakfast since I had a series of patients to see in various places, and my mother remarked: "There's a different look in your eyes. You're more at peace. You don't place so much emphasis on your appearance. You're not obsessed with it anymore. You've gotten better at looking inside. And you can tell what's important from what's not." She said it like that, in the same tone she would have used to give me a grocery list. But her forest-green eyes were damp. Modest, she concealed them, but her emotion was evident. I gave her a hug and, smiling, I murmured, "My sweet Momma Franca . . . "

It was late. I jumped in the car. As I was speeding down the road, the image of Zia Marilena popped in my head. My mother's words had brought her to the surface of my memory. I thought about all our talks. The faith she had in me. I sent her a "Thanks, Zia Marilena!" Zia Marilena had been up in the heavens for a few years now. But I liked to think that she still listened to me when, every once in a while, I talked to her.

14

My evenings were devoted to Ninna. I put her in the outside pen. But I soon realized it wasn't enough for her anymore. In fact, I often found her walking anxiously around the perimeter, as if she were looking for a way out of a prison. I felt terrible for her. So I came up with a solution.

My mother's dogs weren't a danger because they didn't have access to Ninna's corner of the yard. So all I had to do was put Lilly and Jack somewhere in the house—I always carefully avoided any direct contact between them and my baby hedgehog—and that little part of the world became safe. I took Ninna out of the pen and put her on the grass. She explored all around. She seemed so happy after a few nights that it occurred to me to let her go farther. And that was how, armed with a good flashlight, I took up the habit of letting her roam outside the yard, down the dirt road that ran through the fields to the edge of the woods. Our walks lasted hours and hours.

In the silver moonlight, me and her: two nocturnal animals.

Her first steps outside, gracefully circumspect, quickly became little sprints broken up with bursts of hunting. When she came across a smell that attracted her, she planted her little nose on the ground and followed it. First she'd sniff a little to the right, then a little to the left, then in the middle, until, finally certain, she went after her target. She started with a soft sniff: a sort of ff ... ff ... The closer she got to her prey, the harder and faster she breathed: fff, fff, fff, fff. Suddenly, her sniffing stopped and was replaced by the crunch-crunch of little teeth chomping on a beetle or an earwig. Mission accomplished.

Then she'd resume the hunt. I followed. Often, she would stop abruptly in front of me. She'd turn around, looking for me. She'd look at me. Maybe she was waiting for me to catch up? When I moved closer, she resumed walking. We'd get to the edge of the woods, but I didn't let her go in. I was afraid of losing her.

Even though.

Even though Giulia had written me that hedgehogs, when they're strong enough to live on their own, must be returned to their natural habitat.

Huge conflict.

Once I did a test, so to speak, but it was agonizing for me. I was walking behind her on the trail through the fields, on one of those nights full of stars and moonlight. I walked slowly, letting her get farther and farther ahead. When she was pretty far away, I stopped. And closed my eyes.

Ah!

My heart racked with anguish, I whispered to myself: "Go Ninna, go. Run from me. Go and be happy, Ninna. Go, Ninna, go. And may fate be good to you." I stood there suffering, long enough for her to leave. Maybe even a little longer. But by the time I opened my eyes, I was in a total panic. Had Ninna escaped? Would I never see her again? I was shaken up. A tear slid down my cheek. Then I got a hold of myself and looked down at the spot where I'd left her.

Ninna was there! It was unreal! She hadn't gone anywhere! She was turned toward me, waiting for me. Maybe it was the wrong thing to do, but I ran to her and picked her up, electrified at the joy of still having her with me.

My walks with Ninna taught me to listen to the silence of the countryside. That's how I discovered it was anything but. The rustling, the crackling of the leaves, the music of the crickets, the voices of the nocturnal birds, and so much more populated that false quiet. And when I crouched next to my hedgie, who was busy sniffing every square inch of ground, I noticed the frenetic life teeming between those blades of grass. I used my flashlight less and less and grew accustomed to seeing in the dark. Not that well, of course, but enough to make out, on clear and calm nights, the details of that little-big world living there. At times the show was soft, other times more harsh, but always it was fascinating.

On one of our nightly excursions, Ninna and I found ourselves in an adventure I'll never forget. She was farther ahead, as usual, and was busy following a scent. I kept my eye on her. We were at the end of the usual path at the point where the forest began. Suddenly something like a grunt reverberated through the air. Loud. Odd. I had never heard a sound like it. A chill ran over my skin. At the same time, instinctively, I sensed that Ninna was in danger. On impulse, I took my eyes off her to look in the direction of the growl. And the blood in my veins went cold. An enormous badger was running in Ninna's direction, while she continued quietly sniffing, oblivious. As soon as I caught sight of it, I started running toward her, faster than I'd thought myself capable. But it was closer to my hedgie. I was terrified. I flew. My temples were bursting from stress. The badger catapulted into the canal bed alongside our path and clambered up in an instant. It was on her. But by then, so was I. Him, me, and Ninna. Right next to each other. In a flash, I reached out and grabbed my little hedgehog.

Then I spun around, turning my back to the badger, holding Ninna close to my chest to protect her. But not before I saw its jaws splayed in our direction. And the flash of its teeth. It didn't attack me. Maybe it grunted again or snorted. But I don't remember clearly. I'm not sure. It was too much of a shock. But it didn't do anything to me. I just left. The night fell silent. The only audible sound was the beat of my heart. No . . . there was something else, too: Ninna's little heart, next to mine, was just as strong and fast. In unison.

Heart to heart. THUMP, THUMP, THUMP.

Panting, I listened, listening to that frenetic rhythm, and I realized how much I loved that little creature. She and I, as our hearts quieted, returned home nice and slow. Ninna still in my arms. Above, the stars trembled.

15

My father and I had arranged to meet for coffee. We hadn't seen each other for weeks. We sat at a small table next to a large window overlooking the street and started to talk. When we seemed to have caught each other up on everything, we turned to look outside, but without seeing. Then we resumed talking. It was raining. A day the color of the melancholy that had been weighing on me for some time. After staring at a burned-out streetlight on the corner for a while, he turned back to me and said, "You've lost weight." He hesitated for a moment and then, in a worried tone, added, "You look tired. And sad. Is Ninna still with you?"

Tears started to fall down my cheeks, beyond my control. I didn't want to cry, but I couldn't help myself.

"Yes, I still have Ninna. I should set her free, but I can't do it," I stammered, my voice breaking with emotion.

"A wild animal needs to be free, be happy. You have to let her go."

"I tried, once. But she didn't go. She waited for me. It's just that I . . . I've gotten so attached to her."

"How can you be attached to a little wild animal? Ninna's a hedgehog! She's not a dog. Not even a cat."

"I don't think it's that weird to be attached to a hedgehog—"

"Regardless, Massimo, you need to think about her well-being. Not just your own."

My father was right. And his words made me think twice. But I was still conflicted.

Freedom.

What a beautiful word. It has the scent of open fields and the color of the sky. You can breathe it in until it intoxicates you, that blue sky and vibrant grass and boundless space. You can soar in the arms of a soft wind.

My little Ninna, on the other hand, was still in chains.

What scared me about setting her free? That I'd never see her again. But also that she might not make it.

The prison I kept her in was much safer.

She was used to the yard and the surrounding fields. Plus, she had learned to hunt. But that wasn't enough. According to the guidelines, both Italian and international, as Giulia told me, a hedgehog has to weigh at least six hundred fifty grams to be released in the fall. That way, for hibernation, it will have enough fat reserves to stay alive through the winter.

I had read that if you release a hedgehog in spring, it can get by on a weight of five hundred grams, because it will have a long stretch with an abundant food supply, which it can tap into as needed. But that wasn't the case for Ninna. At the end of August, she weighed six hundred grams—enough to free her?

Giulia, at least, had written me:

> You can release her.

Just a couple of words. Four, to be exact. But they made me feel like I'd been run over by a tractor.

Still, my female hedgehog weighed fifty grams below the required weight. If the charts say six hundred fifty, there must be a reason, right? Fifty grams for such a small animal wasn't nothing.

Okay, I confess, I was all too happy to go along with this excuse. I tried to convince Giulia that my little one could actually be considered borderline.

She wrote back:

> I understand your eagerness to protect Ninna . . . but you're not meeting her needs this way.

The message cut me like a knife. But my sadness was partially mitigated by her next two messages:

Massimo, I also feel bad when I release a hedgehog
because I know how much I'll miss it. But at the same
time I'm happy, because I know it will be happy. Every
hedgehog has a right to its freedom.

Massimo, okay, leave Ninna in her pen. She can
hibernate there. Prepare yourself for that separation
first. You'll see her next spring . . .

I burst into tears once again. I was happy that Giulia understood and that my hedgehog would still be staying with me. But
not seeing her all winter triggered more anguish. It was one of
those moments—one cry after another.

Meanwhile, the autumn painted its colors across the yard,
fields, and woods. One evening, on October 14, something happened that surprised me no small amount. My mother and I had
just finished dinner. I went to the window to check on Ninna,
who was outside in her pen. Jack and Lilly were also in the yard.
He was devotedly working on moving a rock, she happily running in circles around him. Illuminated by the yellow lights by
the flowerbeds, they were clearly visible.

I turned to my mother to answer a question she'd asked me,
and when I looked back outside, the two dogs were gone. It was
unusual for Jack to leave a task unfinished. A few seconds later,
they both started barking like crazy. I called them, but they
didn't come. It was the aggressive way they barked when a
stranger entered the garden. A little worried, I thought I'd go

and check. I grabbed a flashlight and went outside. Lilly and Jack, in the back by the fence, right in the darkest spot of the yard, were frantically protesting against something or someone. When I got to them, I noticed nothing out of the ordinary, yet their crazed barking didn't cease. I pointed the flashlight all around, but everything seemed in place. Finally, I managed to quiet them down.

I was about to go back inside when I distinctly heard a sound I knew very well. My heart skipped a beat. My ear, trained by then, had caught the unmistakable *thump thump thump* of a hedgehog's heart beating like mad. "Oh God, Ninna escaped from her pen!" I yelled in the dark. I rushed to the part of the yard where my hedgie was. There she was, busy hunting.

So whose frightened little heart was that, then?

I ran back to where the dogs had resumed their nervous barking. I pushed some flowers aside and parted the bushes. And finally I saw it. It was a frightened hedgehog. I picked it up gently. It balled up, in self-defense. But then it opened a little, enough to show its nose. It was a beautiful creature. It had the sweetest eyes I'd ever seen. What to do? I called for my mother to come and asked her to close Lilly and Jack up somewhere. Then I started exchanging texts with Giulia.

I found a hedgehog in the yard!

Is it big or small?

Smaller than Ninna. Looks like five hundred grams or so.

It's a little close to the weight limit for surviving hibernation, but there's still time. Maybe it'll make it if you feed it regularly.

Giulia, it's a boy!!! :)

Ha! Guess word's gotten around that a pretty lady lives there!!! :)

I set the hedgehog on the ground right where I'd found him and rushed to get him some dry food—kitten chow, which hedgehogs also really like—and water.

But the next night, the little guy was gone. The food and water remained, untouched.

I changed the water so it would be fresh, and replaced the old food with some new.

Several days went by. The hedgehog had vanished. However, sometimes some of the food was gone.

I consulted Giulia once again:

I can't tell if it's the hedgehog eating the food. It could be the neighbor's cat or some other nocturnal animal.

She suggested:

Try putting out pine nuts with it. Cats don't like them. So if they're gone too, it's probably the hedgehog. But also consider the possibility that you won't see him again. He could have just been passing through.

I regretted not keeping him. I would have given him plenty of food to prepare him for the winter. Nevertheless, I kept leaving kitten chow with pine nuts in different spots across the yard. I found a small hole in the fence. Surely that's where the hedgehog had come in. I always put out a little canned meat near it.

On October 26, after dinner, I went to collect the old food and put out some more as usual. And next to the hole in the fence was the hedgehog! My heart leapt with joy. He looked up at me with his sweet little eyes. He didn't move—he had the embarrassed look of someone who'd been caught red-handed. Or maybe he was simply blinded by the glare of my flashlight. Slowly, I reached out and picked him up. His tender, helpless gaze enchanted me.

16

went back inside and weighed the hedgehog. Four hundred fifty grams. I examined him thoroughly to make sure he was all right. His breathing was fast. I thought it was probably due to fear, but I wasn't sure. He had a few ticks stuck in his skin. I passed along this initial information to Giulia. She responded immediately:

> He's a little small. Keep him under observation for a few days, just to figure out what's best to do for him.

The next day—Sunday—Greta came over. Lately, maybe in part because I was still at my mother's, we saw each other a little less. I immediately showed her the new hedgehog.

"You're right, he has the sweetest expression. What a cute little guy! What have you named him?" she asked enthusiastically.

"I found him last night. I haven't thought of a name yet."

"What do you think of Angel Face?"

"Nah, too long."

"Well, since we already have a Ninna, what about Ninno?"

"We're sure imaginative in our choice of names!" I replied, laughing.

She laughed, too. "Oh, come on now. Ninna and Ninno. What a pair!"

Well, after all, I did like the name Ninno.

The hedgehog, or "hedgehoggle," as Greta had cleverly dubbed him, ate the food I put in his cage with a fair appetite. I had carefully pulled off his ticks with tweezers and made sure to remove their heads as well. I didn't use any products, because when a tick is disturbed it releases toxins into its host.

I rechecked every last millimeter of his skin: all clear. So that was one problem solved. But I was concerned about his breathing. I sent Giulia a video.

She replied:

> It's not easy to tell from the video. To be safe, I'd recommend you x-ray his lungs. Ciao.
>
> PS: Even though you've gotten rid of the ticks, it might be good to give Ninno an anti-insect treatment. Choose one hedgehogs can tolerate.

I decided to take the hedgehog to Gianni, a close friend of mine from Asti and a vet who specialized in cats and dogs. He examined him meticulously, inside and out. "In my opinion, he's fine. I don't see any progression of disease. He has no intestinal parasites. The x-rays will be ready in a minute, but they should be normal," he said to me calmly.

"Great! I'll go put Ninno in the car and come back to see the x-rays."

I put him in a little cardboard box in the backseat, gave him a little blanket, and went back in the clinic. Gianni was spot-on: The x-rays proved him right. I told him good-bye and left, completely happy. Back at the car, I went to check on Ninno. His box was empty! I couldn't figure out how it was possible. But he wasn't there. I searched the whole car—backseat, front seat, trunk. And again. And again. Vanished! He couldn't have just evaporated! And the car was locked, so no one could have taken him. I felt like I was in a nightmare. I couldn't wrap my head around it.

What could I do? Well, Ninno was little, and he could have squeezed into who knows where. I would have to check every tiny nook. With mounting worry, I started pulling out all the things I kept in the car. My surgical tool case. The box with all the syringes. Then the metal detector—I use it to find metal foreign objects that animals have accidentally ingested—and the box of magnets. And the thermometer set. And the stethoscope. And the pack of IVs. Two plastic boxes of medications. Artificial insemination sheaths. Ultrasound machine. Esophageal probe. Vaginal probe. Speculum. Bucket. Boots. Can of liquid nitrogen for preserving sperm. Disinfectant. Long-sleeved gloves. Short-sleeved gloves. Plastic shoe covers. Plastic smocks. Exam coats. Extra shirts. Various headwear, including a cowboy hat. An overnight bag with forms for prescriptions and certificates. An iPod I hadn't seen in years. A few dozen veterinary newspapers and magazines. Ninno's empty box and useless blanket. And maybe some other things I don't remember now.

I cleared out the car and littered the ground. All that random stuff spilled onto the sidewalk and the square, undoubtedly creating a surreal scene. But Ninno was nowhere to be found. He couldn't have gotten out of the car! Or could he? Dejected, I looked around, and only then did I realize that six or seven curious people had stopped to watch me. I was upset, but I was still able to see flashes of puzzlement in their eyes.

So I said, "You'll have to excuse me, I hope I haven't created an inconvenience. I'm going to put everything back now. It's just that I lost my hedgehog." My apology garnered a few benevolent smiles. But at "lost hedgehog," my audience suddenly split: One half thought it was an implausible excuse and shook their heads with disappointment; the other half questioned my mental health. A few, just to be safe, stepped away. Overwhelmed by worry, I didn't mind them and instead began telling Ninno's story. How I found him, removed his ticks, how he was too small, how I had taken him for x-rays. "I took everything out of the car, but he's nowhere," I concluded, discouraged.

A girl in a red jacket pointed at a spot in the car and said, "There's one more box back there."

"Yes, but it's locked, he couldn't have gotten in there," I objected glumly.

Nonetheless, I opened it and . . . there was Ninno! He was sleeping peacefully, nestled on top of my scrubs. How had he managed to get himself in there? Shifting things around, I saw the case had a little hole in the back. Happy, I took the hedgehog in my hand and, displaying him like a trophy, shouted at the bystanders: "Found him!" At that, the girl in the red jacket started clapping and cheering. The rest soon followed suit. Big smiles all around, and eyes full of wonder directed at Ninno.

Meanwhile, he'd woken up and was looking up at me sleepily. After petting him gently for a moment, I put him back in his box. Some of the onlookers helped me load all the country veterinarian gear back into the car. When everything was in place, I thanked them and got in the car to return home. Some waved, others yelled good-bye. The girl in the red jacket blew Ninno a kiss.

That same night, I told my cousin Francesco about our little adventure. We both cracked up at the image of me emptying out the car with an audience of onlookers. Well, all's well that ends well.

"I thought of an idea," I said abruptly. "I want to make a park where hedgehogs and other wild animals can live safe and happy."

"Where do we start?" was his pleased response.

I bought a hundred oak saplings, and Francesco and I planted them in a row on the hill near our house on a plot of land my mother owned. That was a step. If Ninna had inspired my dream to create a center for hedgehogs, Ninno had sparked the fantasy of a sanctuary devoted to them.

(Top) It all started with my Ninna, seen here when she was a baby, sleeping peacefully. *(Bottom)* Now fully grown and exploring in a meadow. (*Photos by Massimo Vacchetta*)

(Top) The sweet and timid Ninno. (*Photo by Massimo Vacchetta*)

(Top) Jo, the hoglet without toes. In this photo she had just arrived at the center. *(Bottom)* Trilly, on splendid form, around 1.5 kilos, on the day of his release into the wild. *(Photos by Massimo Vacchetta)*

(*Top*) Selina and Jo. Both are still at the La Ninna center, in a large outdoor enclosure. Their expressions here are very sweet. (*Bottom*) Selina, our dear old woman. (*Photos by Massimo Vacchetta*)

(Top) Zoe. Elderly and missing an eye—which you can't really see in this photo—and with a damaged limb, but despite this quite spry. He is very greedy when it comes to kitten food. (*Photo by Massimo Vacchetta*)

(Top) Taking care of the babies. *(Photo by Esther Amrein)*
(Bottom) The sympathy of Zampa, a disabled hedgehog. *(Photo by Claudio Coccino)*

(Top) Me with my adorable Lisa, the little woodland warrior. *(Bottom)* Carolina. She weighed less than a rosebud when she first arrived. She was so small, she stole my heart. *(Photos by Massimo Vacchetta)*

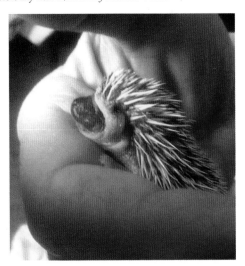

(Top) A baby, only a few days old. *(Bottom)* A week-old hoglet drinking some milk. *(Photos by Enrico Chiavassa)*

(Top) A baby of only 3–4 weeks of age. *(Bottom)* One of the last babies to arrive at the center. She's a naughty little one who's always hungry! *(Photos by Claudio Coccino)*

One of the patients of the center before his release into the wild. *(Photo by Claudio Coccino)*

(Top) Two little orphans saved by the center. *(Bottom)* Three little brothers near weaning. *(Photos by Claudio Coccino)*

(*Top*) A baby of about two months. (*Bottom*) Sissi, a disabled hedgehog who lives at the center. (*Photos by Enrico Chiavassa*)

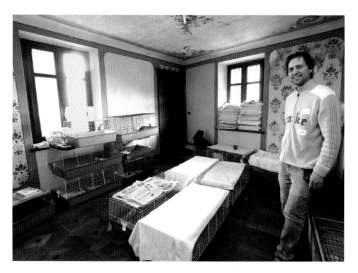

(Top) Part of the La Ninna center, equipped for our tiny guests. *(Photo by Bruno Murialdo) (Bottom)* A bit of relaxation after a good dinner at the center. *(Photo by Enrico Chiavassa)*

(Top) A hoglet: a bout of sleep after eating. *(Bottom)* A post-porridge belly massage. *(Photos by Esther Amrein)*

(Top) Lisa, a piece of my heart. *(Photo by Enrico Chiavassa) (Bottom)* One of two disabled sisters in the center. *(Photo by Esther Amrein)*

The tenderness of Nino. *(Photo by Massimo Vacchètta)*

17

Ninna was eating less than usual. And at night, she was very restless. Agitated.

Once I went over to calm her down. I held out my hand to her. "Ninna, for goodness' sake, calm down!" She stopped for an instant and then tried to attack me. She tried to bite the hand I was holding out to her. I hadn't expected that sort of reaction. It hurt me. But I took her in my arms. I got her to relax, and she seemed to go back to her usual self. However, the same thing happened again several times over the following nights.

She was regaining her natural instincts. She wanted to leave. The song of her sirens was calling her. And she wanted to follow that ancient voice. But by now, it was too late to release her.

Full of pity and guilt: that's how I felt during those drizzly, leaden days . . .

The weather was getting cooler and the nights longer. Fall was ending, and winter was drawing closer. Little by little, Ninna became less active. I reinforced the roof of her house, creating a sort of cavity wall that I insulated with hay. I wanted her to be well sheltered. Ninno, on the other hand, would stay in his cage in my mother's garage. The ideal temperature for him was about sixty degrees. I would keep putting food out for him. He needed to reach a weight of six hundred fifty grams before going into hibernation.

Giulia had written me:

> But Ninna should stay outside. Don't bring her into the house. Temperature changes aren't good for her. You'll see her fall asleep. You shouldn't wake her up. You'll make her waste energy. Hibernation is necessary for hedgehogs. Leave her in peace. You'll see her again in April. Trust her. She knows what to do.

For several days, I thought I really needed to go home. I was happy at my mother's, really. But it didn't seem right to linger. I didn't have an outdoor pen, however, so Ninna and Ninno would stay at her place.

One morning, while we were drinking tea, my mom gave

me a speech: "You can't keep sleeping on that couch. You can't get a decent night's sleep that way. You know what? I'll get a bed. A nice one, a queen. I'll put it in the room next to the living room, and it can be your room." She was radiant, her green eyes shining.

I hated to put out that fire in her eyes, but the time had come. "I have to go back to my place. I went a couple days ago. It was like an abandoned house. I need to turn on the heat and clean up a little." A shadow of sadness was cast over the room.

"Houses fall into disrepair if you're never there," I added in a low voice. I was whispering, I felt like it hurt less that way.

"Massimo, at least come over for dinner. Sometimes," she said, after a long pause filled with lost looks and waves of thoughts. She was pretending not to be so dejected. She put on a cheerful mask and rattled off the dishes and treats she was going to prepare. "Sure, I'll come for dinner. For a while," I stated.

I went to work, leaving my mother to tackle her errands. As if in a hall of mirrors, we left each other with identical little grins, both trying to hide the sadness that had overtaken us.

The next day, Lilly, Jack, and I went home.

Every night, I went to eat at my mother's and diligently tended to Ninna and Ninno. This coming and going was tough on me, though. In the end, I made a decision: I would take the hedgehogs to my place and just go to my mother's a couple of times a week. However, as I mentioned, I didn't have an outdoor pen, only a small enclosure I'd built awhile back that wasn't suitable for the season and their current needs. So I set up two big pens in my attic. It was a large open space with no heat and no furniture. It seemed ideal. I'd take Ninna and Ninno there.

I knew Giulia wouldn't agree. I was sure she'd get mad at me. Thus I didn't write her about the move. I knew I was wrong, so I didn't dare.

Around then, it struck me to put the two hedgehogs together. I wanted them to meet. I was curious to see how they'd act. I hoped they'd become friends and, who knows, maybe fall in love. So I took Ninno and put him in Ninna's pen. I sat for a while and observed them. She took the initiative and started sniffing at him. Then he sniffed, too. They blew puffs of air at each other a few times. She was much more aggressive than he. A shy one, he tried to curl up, roll into a ball, close himself off. She, arrogant and curious, circled him.

After a long time of seeing this scene repeat itself monotonously, I left them to continue their meeting alone and went downstairs to take care of some other things. After a couple of phone calls and a few minutes on the computer to check my e-mail, I distinctly heard one of the hedgehogs huffing very loudly and repeatedly: *fffoo, fffoo, fffoo*. I'd never heard them breathe so forcefully. Were they fighting? I rushed up the stairs and reached the mansard with my heart in my mouth.

I was dumbstruck. I'd been ready for anything, but not that.

No, they weren't fighting.

Nor had romance blossomed between them.

Quite the opposite.

Before my unblinking, incredulous eyes was a sight that makes me laugh again now just thinking of it. A number straight out of Cirque du Soleil! Ninno was completely closed up like . . . a la hedgehog, let's say. A perfect, stiff ball. Ninna, all serious and concentrated, was agilely, gingerly sliding her nose underneath him and then jerking him up, flipping him in the air. And so, she spun the Ninno-ball left and right, up and down, all over the pen. Hilarious! I burst out laughing. I was waiting for her at any moment to add to the performance and jump on top of the ball with an acrobatic bounce and land on tiptoe.

To keep him from getting hurt, I took poor Ninno and put him back in his own pen. There was no love lost between those two. It probably wasn't the season for romance anyway. Later, I discovered that hedgehogs don't couple randomly, but go where their "attractions" pull them. Naturally, boys don't pay so much attention to the details. Girls, on the other hand, seem to be a little more choosy.

Winter dragged on. One night in December, there was a huge snowfall. The next day, everything was buried under a sizable layer of snow. From the attic window, I looked out at that endless white and was happy to have my hedgehogs here with me. Safe. Yes, I know, Ninna probably would have survived regardless. But I was much calmer this way. Ninno ate well and reached a weight of eight hundred grams. At that point, he ate less and started to sleep.

Technically, my two hedgehogs weren't in full-on hibernation, but a proto-hibernation. In actual hibernation, their physiological functions slow down to minimize energy consumption. Their heartbeat and breathing are drastically reduced. In nature, hedgehogs wake up only sporadically and never leave their nest; they just stay there and fall back asleep. Mine only slept for a few days at a time, then woke up and ate a little before resuming interrupted slumber. I checked on them now and then. I was afraid they were dead. So I'd touch Ninna. Irritated, she'd huff at me.

Okay, she was alive.

18

Late February. A gorgeous night, though cold. I was driving fast. Traffic was scarce. I was heading back home from visiting two dear friends, Ezio and Daniela. They were part of the group I'd traveled with to Australia awhile back. In fact, Daniela, who is from Australia, had organized the trip. I was thinking about them and our conversation when I caught sight of something in the middle of the street, lit up by my brights. It took me the tiniest fraction of a second to realize that it was a hedgehog.

What was a hedgehog doing in the middle of the road during hibernation season?

Yet there it was.

I braked hard, but I knew I didn't have enough room to

stop. So I tried to keep my wheels straight so that the hedgehog would be in the middle.

If the hedgehog didn't move, I'd go over without hitting it.

If it didn't move.

There was nothing else I could do.

I drove over the spot where the hedgehog was and turned around. Had I been able to avoid it? I turned on my emergency lights and backed up. When I got closer to that dark spot on the road, I stopped and leapt out of the car. I went over to the hedgehog. I hadn't run it over. Thank heavens! It had stayed there without moving while my wheels passed alongside it. It was very thin—a stripe, a dark rectangle on the asphalt. For a second, I thought that it had been trying to die.

In the distance, I glimpsed the lights of a truck that was rapidly approaching. There was no time to lose. I grabbed the hedgehog with my bare hands and felt its spines pierce my skin. But I paid no attention. I had to get it out of the roadway as fast as possible. I was just in time. The big rig's driver honked madly, a drawn-out explosion that shattered the silent night. It passed me and the hedgehog and then my car. As he and his rage and incessant blaring faded into the distance, I realized I had to move the car. You couldn't stop on the road. There was no shoulder; it was dangerous.

More headlights, still small and far away, headed toward us. I certainly didn't want to cause an accident. I jumped in the car, placed the hedgehog on my legs, and sped away. With one bleeding hand, I held the steering wheel; with the other, just as scraped, I softly pet the hedgehog. As I drove, I glanced down at him from time to time. I felt immensely bad for him.

As soon as I got home, I weighed him. Three hundred eighty grams. Small. I'd expected as much. Then I put him in a cage with an old wool sweater on the bottom so he'd be warmer and more comfortable. Next to it, I left some food in a little bowl. Later, I went to check on him. Unfortunately, he hadn't eaten: Everything was exactly as I'd left it. The hedgehog also hadn't moved an inch. I wrote to Giulia. She replied:

> It's almost certainly had a collapse. Don't give it food.
> You need to warm it up and rehydrate it first.

As soon as I read her message, I set a hot water bottle next to the hedgehog. Then I set up an IV with equal parts 5 percent glucose and Ringer's solution. I took a pair of tweezers and lifted some of the spines in his lumbar region, and grabbed a fold of skin. Then I injected the liquid. The hedgehog had no reaction. Its expression was sad and defeated. I was worried. I took the cage and put it in my room next to my bed.

Awhile later, I was awakened by a strange sound. What was that? My sleep-dulled senses couldn't tell at first. But a few seconds later, it was clear. Coughing. Again. Close by. The hedgehog was coughing like a child. A baby. The coughs started out soft, then grew louder until they faded into a long, exhausted cry. A silent pause and then it started all over again, painfully identical. Besides the cough, sometimes the poor thing would vomit. I quickly wrote Giulia, who passed me on to Gérard. He recommended antibiotics. He told me the cough could be due to lungworm. I should have him checked out as soon as possible.

The following morning, I took the hedgehog to my friend Gianni, and his microscopic examination revealed a large quantity of the parasite's larvae. Transmission usually occurs by ingesting infected slugs or snails. Host and parasite can live in equilibrium, but if the hedgehog gets sick or weak, the lungworm can start to take over and cause serious respiratory illness.

So that was why the hedgehog hadn't gone into hibernation. Or maybe he had, but then woke up due to the cough or, in any case, because he didn't feel well. I quickly began treatment, but he still wasn't eating. Someone suggested I call him Trilly. I don't remember who, but this time it wasn't Greta. I liked "Trilly." It made me think of sweet sounds, fairy tales. I thought it was lovely.

It was Saturday night, and I had plans to go out with friends. Instead, I sat down with the hedgehog and started talking to him. "Trilly, everyone's going out tonight and having fun. Whereas I'm going to stay with you and keep you company, try and help you. Okay? But in return you need to do me a favor. You have to eat. Okay?" He looked at me. When I asked "Okay?" he seemed to pay more attention. Maybe it was the change in tone that made him more alert.

I prepared a special mix. I soaked a handful of kitten chow in water. Then I added a teaspoon of wet cat food. I blended it all together, watering it down a little to make a soft puree, and added a few drops of vitamin B. I drew the mixture up into a syringe. The hedgehog had his back to me. I put the syringe next to his mouth; he promptly turned the other way. I brought the syringe toward his mouth again. This back and forth between his little head and my syringe happened at least twenty times. Left, right, left, right.

Until . . .

During this relay of turns, without meaning to, I squirted some of the food on his nose. At that, Trilly stopped moving his head and started licking his whiskers, his tongue smacking with a rhythmic slurp. He liked my stew. He still had his back to me, but his face was turned in my direction. His eyes were brighter. He seemed to be asking for the food. I slowly depressed the plunger, and Trilly ate. And ate. I didn't force him, I just followed his lead. Had my little speech about Saturday night done the trick, or did he just appreciate my efforts as a five-star chef for hedgehogs? All kidding aside, it was probably the antibiotics starting to take effect, but—if you'll grant me the indulgence—the dish I'd made was still worthy of note!

From then on, Trilly always ate. As soon as he saw me with the syringe of food in my hand, he went wild with joy. Then he started eating on his own from a bowl. The cough and lung-worm proved hard to eradicate, but ultimately they were defeated. Trilly started to fill out and put on weight. At the beginning of summer, he got to one and a half kilos!

Rescuing a little creature in a pitiful state and watching him come back to life was amazing for me. I knew that I'd found my true calling: helping hedgehogs, those little animals that normally don't generate much interest. Helping out, giving. On a Web site for hedgehog fans, I found a reflection that described my state of mind perfectly. I don't remember every word of it, but the gist was this: "None of your days is fully lived until you've done something for someone who can never pay you back." There. That was exactly what I wanted. And what I still want today.

19

The cold season was ending. I spent the long winter nights trying to understand the hedgehog world a little better. I wanted to learn, to understand. I devoured Pat Morris's manual, *Hedgehogs*; Marina Setti's *The Hedgehog: I'm Here Too*; and *Hedgehogs in Veterinary Practice*, the manual put out by the German association Pro Igel. And also *Hedgehog Rehabilitation* by Kate Bullen, and *A Prickly Affair: My Life with Hedgehogs* by Hugh Warwick.

Surfing the Internet, I came upon some very interesting sites: the British Hedgehog Preservation Society; Vale Wildlife Hospital, one of the largest wild animal rescue centers in Europe; Hedgehog Bottom, an English hedgehog rescue center; Pro Igel, the primary German hedgehog association;

and Friends of the Hedgehog, a Swiss organization. I started to interact, participating in their forum discussions, posting question after question. I met Toni and Dorthe, well-known hedgehog experts, the former English and the latter Danish.

Dorthe. Our first encounter was unique. I'd just asked a question on an American hedgehog forum, and right away I received a friend request on Facebook. From Denmark. It was Dorthe. I immediately accepted, and we began to chat, exchanging impressions and notes on hedgehogs. After a lengthy exchange of messages over the course of several days, I received a strange question. Dorthe asked:

Are you a man?

I replied:

Yes, of course.

She typed in response:

Oh God, I've written you a hundred times
thinking you were a woman!!! :)

Simultaneously, we burst out laughing,
she in Denmark and I in Italy. I wrote:

Does it make a difference?

Nooo!!! It's just funny! I mean, it's not funny that
you're a guy! It's funny that I got it wrong! :)

And thus, with ease and a smile, a precious friendship was born. It grew stronger in time and remains today—a friendship made of sharing advice about hedgehogs, of understanding that provides shelter and comfort, of pleasant banter and constructive comparison.

Meanwhile, taking advantage of the nice weather, my cousin Francesco and I set up a large, ten-by-five-meter enclosure in my yard, with a sturdy fence around the perimeter. Inside there was an imposing century-old olive tree that would supply the necessary shade during the warm months. Plus the bushes. And a large rosemary plant. I was satisfied. It was really a nice, functional space. I also dug a few little holes—like mini-burrows—next to the olive tree.

At the beginning of March, I put Ninna and Ninno and their houses in the new enclosure. They seemed happy. When I called Ninna, she came running. Ninno, on the other hand, grew increasingly standoffish and timid, often hiding. I'd find him later in a hole or under the rosemary bush. He'd even climb up it. One time I saw him right on top, perched on one of the highest branches. He seemed like a sparrow. He just sat there all calm and collected, king of the world.

Okay, I know, I shouldn't have put Ninna and Ninno in the same pen. The right thing would have been to keep them separated. In fact, they could have mated and thus reproduced in captivity. And that wouldn't have been good. But when I first started out with hedgehogs, I committed a number of errors, which later I made sure to avoid. Still, I was reassured by the lack of feeling between the two hedgehogs. And it worked out. No mating and no hoglets.

The spring was horrible: torrential rains, incredible storms, little tornadoes. One night there was a frightening downpour that jolted me awake. Water came down in buckets, streams, rivers. Everywhere. Furious wind. Trees uprooted, split, fallen. Thunder resounded like an explosion. Window panes rattled trying to withstand the gusts. There were other, more sinister, less identifiable noises. Lightning broke the darkness in rapid bursts. Pandemonium. The lights even went off—the power had gone out.

I worried that my two hedgehogs, outside, were in serious danger. I rushed to the pen, calling Ninna. I got totally drenched. In a flash of lightning, I saw a hedgehog coming toward me. It was Ninno. I scooped him up and brought him inside the house. I quickly wrapped him in a towel and set him on the rug by the fireplace, where a few logs still glowed. I added some more so he wouldn't get cold. Then I ran back outside to look for Ninna. But she was nowhere to be found. I yelled for her tirelessly, my voice piercing the storm. And nary a trace of her. I didn't give up and went on. I knew her well; I knew she, unlike

Ninno, wouldn't be hiding. I knew when I called, she would come. Where was she then? I was desperate.

After two hours of intense searching, even beyond the pen and outside the yard, I went inside. There wasn't much rain. The fury of the heavens was dying down. I was soaked, the tears running down my face mixing with the rain. Defeated, with death on my mind. What terrible thing had happened to my sweetheart?

I went inside and over to the fireplace. I sat down on the carpet next to Ninno, who hadn't moved an inch. I took off the towel I'd wrapped around him, slowly. And then, by the light of the fire—the power was still out—I saw. It wasn't Ninno! It was Ninna! I hugged her and shouted, "Ninna! My Ninna! It's you! And you're alive!" I was overjoyed. But how could I have mixed them up? I guess with lightning as the only light, and the torrential rain, on that dark night . . . anything could have happened. Add worry, haste, and fear, and you get the picture. Maybe I should have known it couldn't have been Ninno, who never came to me like that.

I cradled Ninna in my arms. In total silence. And inside, I felt happy. I wasn't too worried about Ninno. He always hid. Surely he'd taken shelter. God, my stomach was in knots from getting so upset . . .

The rain stopped. The gray dawn arrived in a whisper, wrapped in a pearl light. I went to the pen. Ninno's little eyes looked up at me from a hole under the olive tree. I gently petted his nose with tiny little strokes. I put Ninna next to him. All was right.

A few days later, I helped my friend Matteo spay a cat. After the operation was over and the kitty was waking up, he and I got lost in conversation. I confided my dream of creating a wildlife preserve where hedgehogs could live happily. It was nice telling him about my fantasies, because he understood them. "Massimo, come with me. We'll take the cat back to her owner, and I'll show you a special place," he said. I smiled. I was curious.

We came to a spot near the Liguria border. The nature around us was spectacular: green hills, calming vales, forest-bordered plains. After reuniting with her cat, Susanna welcomed us with open arms.

Susanna. Big blue eyes. Serene. I was struck by her culture and composure. A former student of Osho, the Indian guru, she spent her time in her house surrounded by roses and raspberry bushes and ancient chestnuts. I told her about my hedgehogs. She said I could release them in her garden when they were ready.

I looked around again. The smells, the peace, the light: It was a perfect place. I was radiant. All three of us were. From

then on, Matteo and I called that place "Paradise." Susanna
told me that there was a property for sale down the road that
would be perfect for a reserve. It was 45 acres of splendor. I
contacted the owner. And thus kicked off negotiations to buy
a dream.

20

I t all proceeded smoothly enough. The spring, too. It was time to launch my center to help hedgehogs in need. I once again called the Wildlife Recovery Center in Cuneo and set up a meeting. On the scheduled day, I went to the office of Remigio Luciano, founder of the center. I knocked, and from inside someone said, "Come in." I went in, then suddenly wondered: Remigio Luciano—which is his first name and which is his last? My slight embarrassment at not knowing how to greet him instantly vanished, replaced by pleasant astonishment at the sight I found: An older man was smiling at me from behind a desk, with an owl perched on his shoulder.

A little owl.

The owlet left its position, hopping onto the desk and then here and there around the room. Then it returned to Remigio's shoulder—yes, Remigio is his first name—and, in vain, tried to climb up onto his head. He allowed it as if it were the most natural thing in the world. At that moment, I thought, "I've come to the right place." And my instincts were confirmed once Remigio showed me around the facilities. Everything exuded love for animals, for nature. And respect.

The complex is located just outside the town of Bernezzo at the foot of a hill. Farther back, mountains frame the setting. The center spreads out lengthwise with pens and cages. Remigio explained to me that they only keep the animals for the time necessary to treat them. When they're healthy, they set them free again. For those with permanent disabilities, they look for other solutions, so the animal can continue its life in the best way possible and with dignity.

We walked along, and I saw animals of every stripe: wolves, deer, fallow deer, chamois, hares, tortoises, badgers, nutria, jays, herons, falcons, eagles, buzzards, and others—and others still. "We also get a lot of hedgehogs," Remigio told me, as he pointed them out in their pens. "We welcome to the center all wild animals who need treatment. We're here to help them. Sometimes they're brought by someone who found them. Sometimes they're reported to us and we go retrieve them ourselves. We're always there to answer the phones and help out, day or night. Some years, something like sixteen hundred animals come through the center. And that's no small number, you know? We need assistance. We have volunteers. But not enough.

There's never enough," he continued. I listened, fascinated.

I told him I didn't like classifying animals as first and second tier, making distinctions between rare and common. He looked out at the horizon and nodded, remarking, "Every living thing has its own importance and unique purpose in the world." We came upon enormous cages, not just wide but extremely tall. "We use these to rehabilitate larger birds for flight," Remigio explained.

I was won over by the place and also by Remigio, who had dedicated his life to helping wild animals. I stopped at one pen, curious: There was a little shed on one side and a deer was coming out. Practically crawling, it came over to the fence that delimited its territory. Close by, it reached out its nose, gently, toward Remigio. Big black and gold eyes, shaded by long lashes. "This is Minerva," he said, greeting her with a tender look. "She's been here since 2004. Look what a proud expression she has! And how elegantly she carries her head and neck, I'd say she has a . . . regal bearing. Yes, *regal* is the right word. I'm not the one who named her Minerva. It was my daughter. I don't name the animals. A deer is Deer, an eagle is Eagle. I don't like giving animals names, because it's a way of humanizing them. At most, to identify them, I might say 'the kestrel with a broken wing,' 'the vulture with the injured beak,' but no more than that."

He invited me to sit with him on a nearby bench, and he told me Minerva the deer's whole story. "She was only three or four days old when they brought her to me. She'd been mangled by a lawn mower. When a baby animal hears unfamiliar noises, it crouches in the grass, thinking it's protected that way. The mother perceives the danger and runs away, trying to get her offspring to follow. But she isn't always successful. Minerva stayed there, unfortunately. And the mower wounded her atrociously. One little leg flew off over the grass. They brought her here along with her severed leg. After urgent aid, I rushed her to the vet. The fawn was anesthetized, and he operated on her from 6 p.m. till one in the morning. Three hundred fifty stitches, external and internal.

"A couple days later, she was already better. She could support herself on her right leg, the one that was reattached. She couldn't on the other. There was a cut tendon that was impossible to mend, and the leg couldn't bear weight. But I was happy. She was saved. I nursed her with a bottle. Day and night. It was just me—at the time, there were no volunteers to take over for me. During the day, she followed me around, even though she limped, while I took care of the other animals.

"One morning two weeks later, I approached the little thing to give her her usual bottle. Everything seemed fine. But I smelled something off. It was like rotting flesh. I was alarmed, so I rushed her back to the vet's. Well, long story short, he had to amputate the leg. We got an artificial limb ready, but it wasn't an easy situation. Plus, Minerva was still growing. What could we do? Put her down because one back leg was missing and the other didn't work? Absolutely not: Minerva wanted to live. So I decided to keep her as she was, and, later, look for a place where she could live happily. I definitely couldn't release her in the wild. With the little strength she had, there was no way she'd survive.

"A few months later, I found a fantastic setup for her. One of our associates who had a home in the mountains agreed to take her in and care for her. I took her over. It would have been ideal for her—greenery everywhere and a comfortable shed built just for her. But Minerva looked at me wide-eyed. Then she started showing signs of nervousness. They grew stronger when I went away and she couldn't follow me. Two days later, I went to take her back. She'd even managed to wound herself, so her stump was bleeding. Minerva missed me, she was very attached to me. As soon as she caught sight of me, she was eager to come to me. And after that, she was my shadow.

"When she was two, I tried again. It failed miserably just like the first time. I resigned myself to the fact that Minerva needed to stay here. By then that was her destiny. It was my fault. I allowed her to get attached to me, compromising her possibility to live a better life somewhere else. I'm sorry for making that mistake. It won't happen again. Here at the center, we take turns bottle-feeding and caring for the animals. This way there isn't one figure taking care of them, and they don't get attached to any one individual, but get used to different people."

I listened to his story attentively. Every so often, I looked over at Minerva, not far away. She was curled up in the grass. She was beautiful. And tame. Now and then her nostrils flared and she seemed to sniff the air.

After a moment, Remigio added, "For me it's important to try and give animals their autonomy. They shouldn't depend on man. Far from it, they should be wary of him, because he's their worst enemy. An animal can't tell a good man from a bad one."

He was giving me wise advice straight from the heart. I understood that. But even though we were both motivated by a great passion for animals, we were different, and for me, in that moment, it was difficult to take in at once. Still, I had lot of material to reflect on. Remigio stood up, approached the deer, and stood there watching her. Then, he suddenly turned toward me and, pragmatically, said, "And now let's move on to the star of the show: hedgehogs!"

21

Remigio and I walked back to his office. He told me, "Before you can start working to take care of hedgehogs, you need a bunch of authorizations." We got to work right away, writing requests and filling out forms. My house in Novello would be an off-site division of the Cuneo Wildlife Recovery Center. "Various officials will come to inspect. And they'll be strict. Rightly so," Remigio said. Only once everything was in order would I receive official approval. We sent the first request to the province. When we finally finished the paperwork, I asked Remigio something that had been rattling around in my head: "How does it feel to release an animal?"

"I've done it more times than I can count. And it's never nice. No, I mean, it's more than nice. Sorry, let me try to explain. The fact is, you always have to think of the animal's well-being. I'll tell you about the last time—that'll make it more clear," he said.

"It was a falcon. As always, I'd checked the atmospheric conditions, thermal columns, the animal's weight and muscle mass. Everything was favorable. So I let it go. It took flight. The higher it rose, the more confidence and speed it seemed to gain. It made circles in the sky. It whipped around, slicing through the air. In that clear blue sky, it searched for the right current. And it found it. With its wings wide and still, it let itself be carried along for a while, like it was suspended. I thought, 'What a wonderful feeling that must be.' And then, it flew off, peaceful. Northwest. Past the trees in the distance. By then it was just a dark silhouette, getting smaller and smaller. A dot on the horizon.

"Well, in that moment, you're happy for it. But at the same time, you also feel this bitterness well up inside. Because it's a separation. And you're consumed with fear, because you know something could happen to it in the future. I'm always afraid freed animals will come to a bad end. And I wish I could know how their lives go on. Once, before freeing a vulture, I had a GPS put on his back, at my own expense. Four thousand euros, not chump change. Yeah, some people might go to the casino and put a figure like that on red or black. I preferred to put it on a vulture's back. We're all free to make our own choices, right? But it's a real satisfaction to know it's alive. And still flying. It'd been rescued in an area of Stura di Demonte Valley. And, when it was time, that's where I released it. The GPS is solar powered, so it recharges automatically. Now that vulture is in Huesca, Spain. At least that's what the latest signal showed."

As Remigio spoke, Carla—one of his most passionate and tireless volunteers—entered the office. She'd heard him telling the story and, turning to Remigio, said, "Tell him about the snake eagle."

"Ah, yes!" he resumed. "We'd rescued a short-toed snake eagle, a big raptor. We treated it. And then we returned it to the wind and sky. Three years later, it was brought back to us. It'd had another accident. We recognized it beyond a doubt by the bracelet we'd put on one of its legs. Healed and back in shape, we released it again. There, I'll say it again, it feels good to know that they go on living."

When we said good-bye and I left for home, the waning sun had already set the sky ablaze. As I drove, I thought back on everything Remigio had said. His parting words echoed in my mind: "Animals are amazing. They're a treasure. All humanity should respect them. And respect nature. Otherwise we'll reach a point of no return. Maybe we already have."

A few days later, the series of inspections began at my house. The gears of bureaucracy had been set in motion. At the start of June, I bought several large cages that I set up in a room of the house. That wing would be devoted solely to hedgehogs. The center was becoming a reality. Choosing a name wasn't hard: La Ninna. It couldn't have been anything else! There it was, the La Ninna Hedgehog Rescue Center.

The permits arrived, signed and countersigned. And then the first hedgehog. One morning Carla, the volunteer I'd met at the Cuneo center, called me: "Massimo, we picked up a dying hedgehog on the side of the road. I think there's little hope of saving it. He's in a bad state, poor little guy. I'll have it brought to your place anyway. Who knows . . ." That hedgehog arrived. Carla was right: It really was in horrible condition. It was a very thin female with dark spines. She lay on one side pretty much motionless and struggled to breathe, her mouth open. Every once in a while, she let out a wheeze. She had, among other things, a very serious case of pneumonia. I did everything I could. I attempted the impossible, initiating a series of specific treatments, and then ran out to get a nebulizer to help her breathe. I spent the rest of the day and the whole night by her side. There was clearly some sort of mycosis around her eyes. She kept them almost shut, but her sad gaze, between those half-lowered lids, pierced my heart.

Dawn hadn't completely erased the dark when the hedgehog showed a few little signs of recovery. Not much, but it fed my hopes. I took some short videos on my phone—which I've kept to this day—to document her condition. Carla called me for news. "She's still with us," I responded. She couldn't believe her ears. She was happy. I added, however, that I couldn't say she was out of the woods. But it already seemed like a miracle. The little thing was also exceptionally infested with ticks. She had them every-where. Over the weekend, Greta came over. I introduced her to

Selina, the sick hedgehog. Yes, I'd already given her a name. I couldn't help it.

My girlfriend and I could have spent our Saturday night having fun together. Instead, we set to work and, one by one, pulled the ticks off Selina. An endless process. Afterward, Greta counted them: over two hundred! They had undoubtedly seriously contributed to bringing the poor thing down so low.

The days passed, and Selina improved, finally able to stand up on her own. Once she was in good shape, I put her in the pen outside with Ninna and Ninno. Selina and Ninna challenged each other a little, huffing and puffing. After establishing that she was the older and more experienced one, and therefore owed a certain respect, Selina began to build her nest. It was extraordinary: She took the hay in her mouth and then arranged it masterfully under the rosemary bush—to and fro for a while, as she moved slowly, until the job was complete. A stupendous nest, with one opening at the base and another at the top.

Selina was at peace roaming around the enclosure. Sometimes, although it was hard, she climbed onto the roof of Ninna's house and looked around from there. I was happy. The first hedgehog to arrive at the La Ninna center was safe and sound!

22

Meanwhile, what had happened to little Trilly?

He was still there, at the La Ninna Hedgehog Rescue Center. Healthy and plump. One day I did a test. I put him in the outdoor pen with Ninna, just to see how he would behave. I was pleasantly surprised. He was immediately attracted to Ninna and began circling her. He'd always been so difficult and ill-tempered, but with her he showed an unexpected patience and tenderness.

It was captivating.

She was cautious but not distrustful. Almost totally still, she looked at him now and again with her bright little eyes. Trilly courted her elegantly, subtly. It was unbelievably kind and sweet. When Ninna gave off some subtle hints that she wasn't rejecting him but rather was pleased to accept his attentions, I decided to separate them, fearing that love could blossom any moment. I set up a divider in part of the enclosure and put Trilly there. That way he could still live outside, and get used to feeling the grass and leaves under his feet and the sky over his head again. He kept getting bigger and stronger. And as I'd anticipated, he even reached a weight of one and a half kilos.

Yes, the time had come . . .

I'd prepared a new, very nice little house for him, again using an old wine crate. It came out a masterpiece, with a little trough, built like the house, with a ten-by-ten-centimeter opening. The food went in the opposite side from the entrance so that cats couldn't steal his chow. And, speaking of chow, I remember I'd offered a special menu that night, with various types of kibble and pieces of meat. And a slice of watermelon.

I didn't want him to forget.

But who knows . . .

Because this was to be our last night together. The following day, I was taking him to Susanna's, to the place that by now all my friends knew as "Paradise."

And there, I was going to free him.

The next morning, the unveiled sun announced a splendid day. It was a pleasant temperature. But I felt so strange. Sure yet undecided, in alternation. I was afraid I'd never see Trilly again. But my desire to let him live his life in complete freedom was stronger. And that gave me joy. Yet it was a joy colored by the fact that I missed him already.

Everything was ready. I reached into Trilly's house to pick him up. He bit me. Hard. My finger was bleeding. "Blood. That's how you seal a pact. A rite of brotherhood. So a friendship will last forever," I found myself telling him, with a melancholy smile.

We left. I drove very carefully as I didn't want him to get nauseous—I'd learned my lesson from that trip to the sea with Ninna. Moreover, I wanted everything to happen slowly. I felt the need to face the journey not just as a physical one, but also as a more personal, spiritual path.

Inside the car, it was Trilly, me, and the magical notes of Ludovico Einaudi. I'd chosen the music carefully. It was the most appropriate for that moment.

Valley after valley led us to a ridge. From there you could see Paradise. I stopped the car and got out for a minute. Savoring that vista, every bit of it, I felt good. Sky, earth, mountains, grass, trees, birds in flight—uncontaminated harmony. There could be no more beautiful place for Trilly, and for a moment I felt at peace.

When we got to Paradise, Susanna greeted us. Her white hair was gathered at her nape. She wore a light, three-quarter-length dress. It billowed gently with the breeze and then softly fell. She was holding a book, with a finger between pages keeping her place. As always, her eyes and smile were serene. And sincere.

We walked through her beautiful, partially unkempt yard to the guest house where she invited friends sometimes. It was stone, surrounded by ivy and other creepers. Near there, in the shadow of a laurel hedge, I set Trilly's house, with him in it, and the trough. And a bowl of fresh water. I did everything with ease, followed by Susanna's light eyes. I turned to her and said: "I think everything's in order. Remember to make sure he always has food and water. And tonight, when you get a chance, check on him, just to see whether he comes out." I'd brought Trilly there early on purpose, so he'd have plenty of time to orient himself and figure out where his food and water were before night fell and he went out to explore.

Then it was time for good-bye. "Bye, Trilly. I'm leaving you here, in Paradise. Take care of yourself. Good luck."

I started for the car. Before leaving, I waved good-bye to Susanna. She waved back, while one of her cats tried to catch a fluttering strip of her dress.

I'd found Trilly in such miserable condition, and now he was strong and healthy.

And free.

I was so happy for him!

The next morning, I called Susanna. I wanted news, to find out how the first night had gone. She replied, "I don't know whether Trilly is still in his house or if he's out. I watched until late, but he didn't come out."

"What? Were you there watching the whole time?" I asked her.

"Yes. I took a seat and planted myself directly in front of his house. I had a flashlight, and every so often I pointed it at it. But I never saw him," she confirmed.

"But if he senses your presence, he won't come out," I said.

"Oops . . ." she said.

We both broke out in laughter, imagining Trilly impatiently waiting for her to get tired and go off to bed so he could finally come out.

The next day, I went back. Trilly was gone. But that wasn't the end of it. Several times during the summer, Susanna noticed a huge hedgehog. She wasn't completely sure, but I felt it was Trilly. Such large hedgehogs aren't common. She'd see it in the late evening, in the yard, near the house and surrounding area. And, naturally, around the trough. But the best part was in August, because something strange happened. Which, when I really think about it, isn't so strange: baby hedgehogs! Tons of 'em. I went to visit. I wanted to bring her some kibble and chat. Talking with her was always pleasant and interesting. And so I saw all the hoglets, too.

I'm sure a fair number of that overabundance of hedgehogs was Trilly's offspring. I would have bet on it. After all, hadn't I seen him in action with Ninna? I knew that lady hedgehogs couldn't resist his charms!

23

By now the La Ninna Hedgehog Rescue Center was open for business. Hedgehogs came from all over. Mostly babies, but also wounded adults. Looking after them all started to become a lot of work. Luckily, I had some volunteers to give me a hand. How did I find them? Well, it actually happened by chance. Like one afternoon when the phone rang. I answered immediately. On the other end, a girl's excited voice. "I found two baby hedgehogs. I know for sure they haven't eaten in at least two days. I don't know how to help them. Can I bring them to you?" An hour later, she came over with her entire family. In one hand, she held a box with the hedgehogs. She offered me the other: "I'm Patrizia. I called a little while ago."

I took care of the little ones right away. First thing, they needed to be rehydrated. Meanwhile, Patrizia told me how she found them. "Two days ago, we saw a dead hedgehog on the road in front of our house. I don't know why, but right away we had the impression she was a mother. We felt so bad for her. So we decided to bury her in the yard. And today, in the sun, right where we'd buried her, there were these two babies. Had they smelled the hedgehog underground and wandered there because of that? Or maybe their nest was nearby? Or maybe they were just hungry? We don't know. The fact remains, there they were. And it seemed like they were looking for something. Or someone . . . And we wanted to help them. Our vet gave us your number. He told us you rescue hedgehogs here."

"Yeah, we're getting famous," I said, smiling. I'd almost finished with the hoglets. "They weigh eighty grams each. And there's a good chance they'll survive. Leave them here. I'll keep you updated on their condition."

"I like how you handle them. Gentle yet confident," Patrizia remarked, pleased.

"Helping hedgehogs is very important to me. They're such defenseless little creatures. And often overlooked. I think they're special. As is every creature in this world, anyway."

Thus, we said good-bye.

But the next day, Patrizia called me again, worked up. "I found another baby hedgehog. In the same place."

A little brother who'd gone an extra day without food. There was no time to waste. I met her halfway and, once I got back, immediately treated the third orphan.

Day by day, the three hoglets grew. Patrizia and her parents frequently came to visit and each time were astonished at their progress.

The little foundlings quickly reached the ideal weight for being returned to their natural habitat. Also, they were healthy; they'd just needed to be adequately nourished. Patrizia and I took them into the hills. Far away, to some friends. A "pre-release" pen had been specially built for them, where the three siblings would have a chance, under proper supervision, to adjust. Two weeks later, we opened the gates and freed them completely. Choked up with emotion, we watched them take their first steps and then dash off into the grass, through the shrubs, unconfined. Mission accomplished!

"You're smiling. But not with your eyes," Patrizia said to me. "There's a big shadow there. You're happy and sad." And that was exactly how I felt.

She understood.

So I ventured to ask, "What made you so concerned about those little hedgehogs?"

"It's an old story."

"Maybe this is the time and place to tell it."

"It was May 29, 1999, when I held a hedgehog in my hands for the first time. Not a real one, it was a stuffed animal. A friend had given it to me. Because I talked so little. I kept everything inside—closed myself up like a hedgehog, he said. In fact, he even called me 'hedgie.' From then on, people often gave me hedgehog gifts, other friends or relatives, until I had a whole collection. I had all kinds: glass, silver, wood. And when I saw those three real hedgehogs in the garden, flesh and blood, and their dead mother . . . well, something clicked."

I nodded. She was silent for a moment, her gaze lost on the horizon, chasing memories. Then she continued: "I've always loved all animals, and my secret dream was to be able to do something for them. Those three hoglets ended up on my street. That means it was fate. And there's something else, too. Your enthusiasm is infectious. I want to find a way to help hedgehogs, too."

It was a poignant moment. The air was charged. The three hedgehogs' release and now such a genuine, selfless offer of help. I concealed how emotional it made me with a smile and a few words. "You're in!" I said.

She laughed, happy. "But I don't live near town. What can we do?" We both knew that when there's passion and goodwill, you find a way. And so it was. Patrizia is still an active volunteer. She works remotely, handling social media for the La Ninna center—for example, our Facebook page, where she replies to requests for help, giving information or directions to the nearest rescue center. She sets up our stand at events and prepares our informational/instructional items, conducts giveaways, keeps up with our contacts, and much more. She's priceless! And like her, there are several others. Volunteers who share my work and the passion, my joys, pains, and hopes.

That summer I released lots of hedgehogs. Always in beautiful spots. I didn't take them to Susanna's anymore, to avoid over-populating the area, since Trilly had already taken care of that.

But I still had Ninna. I couldn't manage to pull away.

Even though.

Even though I thought about it all the time. And every time I did a release, I felt guilty. I gave other hedgehogs their lives back, but not Ninna. Giulia wrote me so:

> Let her go!

Dorthe, my Danish friend, also insisted:

> The right thing is for Ninna to go her own way. She's healthy, and it's her right. And you'll have more room, more time, and more energy for the other hedgehogs arriving at your center. And for others in the future. Massimo, don't listen to that little part of yourself controlled by selfishness. You're not a selfish person.

They were right, oh yes, they were right! But it was so hard.

24

That summer Salvo arrived. A girl had found him in her yard. She'd taken care of him for a few days, but when she realized the hedgehog's condition was getting worse, she asked the Wildlife Recovery Center in Cuneo for help, and they sent her to me.

I examined it closely. It was in a terrible state. Its front legs were paralyzed. The back ones barely moved, almost not at all. She'd name him Salvo, perhaps out of the wish he'd be saved or maybe because he'd managed to survive so far.

The hedgehog had signs of a serious neurological problem. The episodes would happen suddenly. At their height, his mouth would spread into a grimace. A clear symptom of his condition, I knew. But it also looked like a desperate, mute cry for help.

A silent scream.

Which infused me with a dizzying dose of worry.

During these fits, at a certain point, Salvo would twist his head back and jerk up and down—up, down, up, down, up, down—fast, uncontrollably.

I told the girl the situation was rough. Her eyes glistened. She didn't hide it. She wasn't embarrassed. She was totally gripped by Salvo's tragedy. Her voice shaking, she whispered, "Do whatever you can, please."

I tried to assess objectively, even though a part of me was already emotionally involved. In my heart, I hoped for a miracle, because I wasn't sure treatment would cure his symptoms enough for him to be returned to nature. For an exact diagnosis and prognosis, we needed sophisticated tools, like a CT scanner, that we don't usually use.

I talked to Dorthe on the phone. She said, "If it doesn't respond to treatment, improve, you have to ask yourself whether it would be right to let it live like that."

It was a difficult, endless subject. Indeed, what sort of life could that hedgehog have if it couldn't walk or run?

I also discussed it with the girl who'd found him. "If he can be saved, but can't live on his own, I'll keep him forever. I'll make him a pen in my yard and feed him. And if I have to spoon-feed him every time, I will," she said.

I wished I could ask Salvo, "Would you rather live or die?" And most of all, I wished he could answer me.

What a dilemma! In any case, I decided to try. It could be worth the effort, because Salvo's condition was the effect of a cranial trauma. Also, in my twenty years of experience as a veterinarian, I'd seen other seemingly hopeless cases turn out surprisingly well. So for Salvo, I followed the protocol recommended by the Vale Wildlife Hospital for cases like his.

I find that euthanasia is the last step, one I never want to take. Because it's excruciating. I can only justify it when there's not even a glimmer of hope. Only when the situation is really completely compromised. Only when there's no other possible treatment, and only when it spares needless pain and suffering. Only out of mercy.

I think that even a disabled hedgehog has a right to live. Sure, it might not be able to run and hunt and be independent, but if it's not in physical pain, why stop it from living in a way that's "different" but good nevertheless? The ideal would be to house these "dependent" hedgehogs with people willing to take care of them with attention and love. It's true that a hedgehog, like any wild animal, should be free, but it's also true that there are hedgehogs that choose to live their whole life in a single backyard.

One of my dreams is to create a place just for disadvantaged hedgehogs, on that plot of land I'd bought that summer near Susanna's "Paradise." It's another paradise.

Yes, "one of my dreams," because I have many others. For example, even more corners of nature to preserve, for hedgehogs and other animals, and for oak trees, beech trees, chestnut trees, and hawthorn . . . One dream after another. A herd.

I had to hand-feed Salvo myself for him to eat, or put the food right next to him, right under his nose.

His ability to move was zero.

That night when I went to bed, I took him with me so I could keep a closer eye on him. I didn't want anything to happen to him without my noticing. I put some pillows on the opposite side of the bed so he wouldn't fall. When I woke up the next morning, he was closer. He had dragged himself toward me. Maybe he was looking for warmth. I opened my eyes and saw his, meek and melancholy, staring at me.

One night, as I'd feared, he grew markedly worse. He was dying. I was devastated. I called Dorthe. And she helped me through it. With her extraordinary sensitivity.

She said, "Don't let him die alone. Let him feel your love. Your warmth. Take him in your hands and pull him to your chest. Keep him there. Until he's gone."

I put him next to my heart. I held him with both hands. I felt a terrible sensation, because I could truly, distinctly sense his life dwindling, leaving him. His head twitched yet again.

For an instant, I'm sure of it, he looked at me. Then a sigh. Soft.
His last.

Poor, dear, little Salvo. We'd failed. Maybe he'd won me over because he was disabled. A handicapped hedgehog has something special.

Overcome with despair, I called Dorthe again. And she was there to console me.

At the end of August, Jo arrived. Another, even bigger challenge. She was a baby. Her back and hind legs were wounded. A dog had mauled her. As if that weren't enough, she was also very small. Seventeen grams. Less than Ninna when I met her for the first time. Less than a silk handkerchief. Less than a veil. I snapped some photos and sent them to Giulia. She wrote:

It's really very small. Massimo, you'll need a lot of luck.

I started to treat her with a suitable antibiotic. I came up with some unbelievable dilutions to give her an appropriate dose for her weight and her condition. Jo responded well. And she had an appetite. And she grew. I remember when she finished her milk, she would fall asleep in the palm of my hand. It made me smile with tenderness. Then I set her very softly on a cashmere throw someone had given me as a gift, and she snuggled up between the folds. As she grew, it became clear that the toes on her back feet had necrotized. A line of dark tissue formed, and then they fell off. All at once.

So Jo lost her toes.

It was a handicap that would preclude her the possibility of a life of freedom. She was very sweet and very affectionate. And I loved her more every day.

Dorthe didn't give up:

> Massimo, maybe Jo fell out of the sky just for you. She'll probably stay with you forever. And I bet she will help you detach from Ninna, ease your suffering, fill the emptiness.

But I, for my entire life, had always tried not to let go . . . I never had the strength.

At the thought of releasing Ninna, I was again seized by a vague feeling of abandonment. A stifling sadness that clouded everything.

25

thought about it. Constantly. Without coming up with anything concrete. And then suddenly, in the first days of September, the decision came.

In a flash.

Tomorrow was the day.

To release Ninna. And Ninno.

I slowly worked out a plan, and every last detail was clear. I would leave them at Susanna's house, in Paradise.

I couldn't bring myself to think that we'd never meet again. It would have been impossible, or at least unacceptable, for my mind to conceive of such an idea. Not seeing her ever again was just an abstract image for me, unreal. Ninno, maybe him I wouldn't see again. As I've said, he was more shy—he tended to hide and didn't respond to my calls. But not her. She would come.

At first, I thought of releasing Ninna in the grove near my house. That way there would be more of a chance of running into her. But a street runs along the perimeter, so it was dangerous. Yes, Paradise was better.

Ninna was stressed. At the beginning of spring, she was eating abundantly, but now she ate less. Cranky, she huffed at the other hedgehogs, and no one dared come close anymore. She even huffed at me. She was fitful. Dorthe said, "If she goes on like that, one of these days you're going to find her dead." And that was precisely what I didn't want. It would have made me too upset. Actually, I thought if I let her go, I'd never know when she died. That way, in my heart, she would go on living forever, running through the fields, hopping, hunting bugs, hiding, having babies, going into hibernation in winter, and waking up in spring.

By then, I'd released many hedgehogs. And I'd seen their eyes sparkle like bright stars when they realized they were free. In the moment, those little creatures oozed happiness from every quill and hair. I wanted that same happiness for her, for my Ninna.

Those releases, for the most part, were preceded by a kind of preparation, so that the hedgehogs could get settled, the same as we did with the hoglets Patrizia had found. An enclosure set up in the place chosen for the release, a few weeks under observation, and then . . . out! And I liked that method. But it wouldn't be ideal at Susanna's, a wonderful place but more remote. Predators could come from the nearby, immense forest, and in a pen, Ninna and Ninno would have no chance of escape. So I'd do the same thing I did for Trilly.

I prepared them two new houses. Big, nice, functional. I'd even insulated them. I also bought a large house to make into a trough.

And that night, as I did before every release, a five-star dinner with a side of pine nuts.

The following morning, I went to the enclosure outside. I started calling, "Ninna, Ninnaaa . . . " in a slightly disguised voice, the singsongy sort you'd use with a child. She popped out of the opening of her house. She looked at me with sleepy eyes. I extended her some food and filmed her as she ate. My last memory of her at my house. I put her in her new place, with a little of her old hay so that she would have her scent. And I left her there. She fell asleep, calm.

Now it was Ninno's turn. It would be harder with him. He often burrowed down in a hole by the olive tree. In fact, that's where I found him. But I couldn't get him to come out. The opening of the burrow was narrow, and Ninno was big. He'd gotten huge like Trilly. Entering and exiting spontaneously was a breeze for him, because he could shrink down by stretching and flattening out. Without his collaboration, it was impossible.

I had to dig a little around it to widen the hole. For a moment, I felt like I was doing him wrong; after all, he was fine there. He had never shown signs of restlessness. But who knows. In the end, I put him in his house, and once I loaded the car, we left.

As in a screenplay, this time I carefully chose the soundtrack that would accompany us on our trip: some music by an American band I'd heard a few days before on the radio. I don't remember their name, but the feelings it sparked, those I remembered. Sweet notes that touched my heartstrings and brought me back to childhood stories and nursery rhymes. Sounds that pleased the child still inside me.

It was a slow drive, with several stops. For Ninna and Ninno. I didn't want them to get carsick. And for me. To extend that time with them as much as possible. When we arrived, I looked around for a moment. It was clear, this was truly a fantastic place. And I was happy for my hedgies.

Susanna was there waiting for me, with her usual serene smile. We headed straight for the guesthouse, then went a little farther, past a small field and some rosebushes. We stopped in front of a little log cabin that had been built years ago for her grandchildren to play in. But they'd grown up, and no one used it anymore. It had windows, a door, a roof. On the bottom of the door, there was a wide slit that seemed created specifically for hedgehogs to pass through. It was all perfect. A little farther on, there was a majestic weeping willow. Behind it, blackberry bushes. On the right, a stack of wood. Good hiding spots. I set the hedgehog houses, with the two inside, in the children's log cabin.

Cabins in the cabin.

I finished setting up the trough nearby. It was a beautiful day, and in that natural setting vibrating with life, it was even more so. There was a to-and-fro of butterflies, dragonflies, bees, birds, lizards, and so on. I stayed at Susanna's for dinner. "That way we'll see if Ninna and Ninno come out," she said. In what seemed to me like an instant, the sun set and the first shadows of the evening appeared. We ate quickly and rushed to check on the two hedgehogs. I reached right into their houses.

Empty.

I wish I could have seen her come out.

I wanted to see her happiness.

I heard a rustle behind me. I spun around, pointing my flashlight. It was Ninno. I stroked his back.

Of her, no trace.

I stayed for a while longer. Susanna stayed with me. "May they enjoy their first night in Paradise," I said, breaking the silence that had fallen.

A moment later, I told her good-bye. I returned home, driving very slow.

I was strangely happy. Very happy. For Ninna and Ninno.

26

On the way back, at points, that feeling of happiness started to crack. I felt a little like a father, or mother, when they leave their kids, now grown, to find their own way. You're happy for them but worried at the same time, because you won't be able to protect them anymore. And you know the dangers they could run into. And you're scared.

If only I could follow Ninna, at least to keep her from badgers . . .

As soon as I got home, I was swept up in another reality: I had to feed all the hedgehogs there waiting for me. And tend to them. I got to work swiftly, but when I reached the pen outside, I stopped cold. At that moment, it really hit home that my hedgie was gone. And she wouldn't come running to me anymore. The silence around me and the despair I felt weighed heavily on me.

And I felt the emptiness.

But I immediately erased that thought.

The emptiness was just mine, and it didn't matter.

Ninna was happy. And that was everything.

I didn't move for a while, as if bolted in place. Minutes filled with thoughts: I did it! I got through it. I freed her. It's incredible that I had the nerve. It's incredible, given how I am. There, that's what love is. Dorthe was right: Loving is letting go.

I was distracted by a soft rustle of grass and leaves. It was Selina. She had gone to Ninna's house and was sitting in front. She looked at the doorway. Then she looked at me. Then again at the doorway. And then me. It seemed like she was asking, "Where's Ninna?" It was written in her eyes, in her movements. After their initial tiffs, once the hierarchy was established, she and Ninna had lived together harmoniously. Maybe Selina felt her absence, too. That action touched me. We both missed her.

I called Dorthe. I needed some comfort. "Go to Jo and give her a big hug." I went to Jo. Now she, without her hind toes, was the one who needed me. I pulled her sweetly to my chest. Nostalgia and consolation blended together. And thus, the former was softened.

Ninna left room for the other hedgehogs. But she would never leave her place in my heart. It would always have a special spot for her.

In the days that followed, I wanted to go back to Susanna's, but a litter was brought to the center. The babies needed to eat every three hours, so there wasn't time.

"There's activity," Susanna told me. "Lots of hedgies come to eat and drink. But I don't know if Ninna is one of them."

I wished I could go and stay there an entire night. When I finally managed to find the time, I had to content myself with just an evening. It was a busy one, though: Hedgehogs upon hedgehogs of all sizes and all ages scurried around Paradise. But no Ninna. She didn't come. Had she found Trilly? Could their love finally bloom? Who knows. Well, it was possible. The silver moonlight fell, soft, on this thought and my smile.

27

The summer was ending. The first leaves to become spotted with red and yellow and rust orange suggested as much. As did the cool air.

It was sunset when the telephone rang. "Hello, La Ninna center," I said.

On the other end, a little girl said, "I found a sick hedgehog. Can you help him?"

"Bring him over right away."

Sofia—that was the girl's name—had her mother tell me on speakerphone what happened.

"We were walking along the river, and on the gravel road parallel to the path we were on, but a little farther down, we saw a hedgehog. It wasn't moving. Sofia ran to help it like she had winged feet. But a car, a big four-by-four, was coming. We had stayed back, and we were scared and told her to move, to get away from there. But her only response was to plant herself in front of the hedgehog and raise her hands, with her fingers all spread out to tell the driver of the car to stop. You had to see it—a girl so little but so determined, in front of that off-roader."

"Oh, I can imagine! Sofia, you're a hero," I exclaimed.

"They wanted to squash him!" the girl said in a little voice, sounding like an indignant angel.

"Squash him?" I echoed, disconcerted, seeking confirmation.

"Yes. And I protected him."

That little girl's gesture stole my heart. I was touched by her courage, her swift reaction, her spontaneity.

The mother went on. "The guy who was driving slammed on the brakes. They stopped a few yards from my daughter. They rolled down the windows and were pissed off, yelling, 'What are you thinking, jumping into the middle of the road like that?'"

Sofia intervened again. "I told him there was an animal that couldn't move. And they yelled back, 'Can't you see it's half-dead?' and I replied, 'So? Since it's dying, you want to squash him with your big fat wheels? At least let me move him, then you can go.' Meanwhile Mom and Dad had come down, and they helped me move the hedgehog over to the side of the road."

I followed the story attentively, at the same time picturing the whole scene in my mind, and I took consolation from that little girl who had rebuked grown-ups to defend the defenseless with her whole heart. Sofia had sent a big message, with all the rawness and sincerity of her feelings. Children, in their simplicity, can teach those of us who have forgotten or never wanted to learn. Those who don't know compassion.

And I felt that maybe, my hope for a better world wasn't just an illusion.

A world without violence and without indifference.

"Hello, Doctor? Are you still there? Can you hear me?"

"Yes, yes, I'm here! Sorry, Sofia, I got lost in my thoughts for a second. I'm listening."

"Doctor, can you save this hedgehog?"

"I'll give it all I've got. I'm expecting you."

They arrived a while later, the time it took to travel the many kilometers dividing us. When I opened the door, I found the whole family. In front, Sofia. About eight years old. Blond curls and sapphire eyes as big as lakes. In her arms was a box, and in the box the hedgehog. My welcoming smile dissolved as soon as I saw him: a dirty rag barely holding on to his last seconds of life.

I examined him carefully. The minutes went by, and Sofia's blue gaze never left me. Whereas I tried to keep my eyes down, so the girl wouldn't see the bitter truth.

"Is it serious? Can you save him?" she asked abruptly. Her voice vibrated in my eardrums. I had to answer. I didn't want to disappoint her, nor did I want her lovely gesture to seem futile. But I couldn't lie. "It's serious, but I'll do what I can," I said.

It was getting late, and Sofia's parents said they needed to go. I accompanied them to the door and down the stairs. They were at their car when Sofia exclaimed, "Just a second, please!" And she dashed off. Nothing to do but follow. I saw her pet the hedgehog softly. We were enveloped in a silence no one dared break. Still silent, the girl turned her giant eyes to mine, a sea-colored gaze that spoke to my soul.

"You can go, Sofia. Don't worry. I'll update you tomorrow," I told her, already thinking about what words to use the following day so she wouldn't be too hurt.

They left, and I found myself face-to-face with the hedgehog on his last legs. He had a series of grave disorders and also was blind in one eye and had one front leg half-mutilated. I wanted to save him at all costs because Sofia's sensibilities and efforts were involved. But also for him: He had managed to survive in nature, at least so far, despite his serious disabilities— his leg and eye injuries were preexisting, old and already healed.

It seemed like an impossible mission.

I spent the night taking care of him, the hours marked by the nearby bell tower. I started a few different treatments but didn't see the least improvement. Around 5 a.m., I realized there was nothing more I could do for him. I gave him a blanket and set a towel over one side of the box so the light from the imminent dawn wouldn't bother him. Then I put him at the foot of my bed, so he wouldn't be alone.

Despite his loud and tortured breath, so like a death rattle,

I slept like a log. I was exhausted. I woke up two or three hours later with a start. I sat up in bed and realized that the room was totally quiet. Too quiet. That strained breath beating my ears and heart was gone.

So the hedgehog was dead.

How would I tell little Sofia?

I reluctantly got up and went over to the cardboard box. I removed the towel. And then the blanket covering the hedgehog.

I rubbed my eyes.

That rumble was gone because his breathing had become regular.

Happy! I felt happy for him, for Sofia, for me.

The hedgehog, albeit slowly, had reacted well to my treatments.

I called him Zoe, from the Greek word for "life." Because, after all, it was like he'd been reborn. His recovery, I admit, cost me great sacrifice. I had to spoon-feed him—he couldn't eat on his own. But at least when Sofia called, I was able to give her good news. And I liked that.

During that period, there was a volunteer who came to help me out. She was a lovely woman, of a certain age, small and petite. At every moment, shaking her head, she'd say, "Zoe won't make it. It's impossible."

"Have a little faith," I would exhort.

A month went by when one morning, I saw him eating on his own. I always put a plate out for him with a little kibble, hoping to encourage him. I called the volunteer, who was taking care of the other hedgehogs. "Come quick, you have to see this."

She came and started looking around. "What's going on? What am I supposed to look at?"

I picked her up and aimed her at Zoe's cage. "You see now?"

"Oh! All the saints in heaven! Zoe is eating on his own! He did it! You did it!" And as she was still in my hands, she laughed and laughed. We both laughed, content.

Now he lives here at the center, in an outdoor pen. His advanced age and his handicaps won't allow him to live freely in nature. He sleeps in a hollow trunk on a bed of hay. He's doing well. He eats, wanders around his own way, looks at the stars.

Zoe was adopted remotely by Valeria.

Awhile ago, the volunteers and I had started a campaign for long-distance adoptions, reserved for disabled or sick hedgehogs. Everyone who does this kind of adoption receives a certificate, the hedgehog's ID card, documentation of its history, and an update on its condition. Naturally, adoptive parents can come and visit whenever they like, and come along if and when it's being released. We like to do it together. To share the experience.

Realizing another dream of mine, we got a special permit to arrange adoptions, under our supervision, of permanently disabled hedgehogs. They would go to people who meet certain requirements. They live good and dignified lives in their pens, in appropriate yards.

My mother adopted one, too.

My mom isn't doing well. She has chronic pulmonary emphysema, and she's constantly attached to an oxygen tank. She has a primary one installed in the house and a smaller one for walking around.

It's very difficult for her to move, and every breath costs her. But in the pen in the yard, there's this handicapped hedgehog. And she, overcoming her own disabilities, goes to him with her tank and takes care of him with attention and love.

Like little Sofia, my Momma Franchina has a big heart. You can learn a lot from big hearts. They know how to give in a heartbeat.

28

The days added up, and the months, with other hedgehog stories, new joys, and new struggles.

It was February when a woman called. She told me she needed help.

"I have a female African hedgehog that's not doing well," she explained.

"I don't have any experience with African hedgehogs, only European," I said. "You should consult a veterinarian who specializes in exotic animals."

"I don't know of any," she replied. "My hedgehog gave birth to a hoglet five days ago, and since then she has been bleeding quite a lot."

"Bring her over right away." To avoid losing precious time,

A HANDFUL *of* HAPPINESS

I would consult some experts myself. That little lady needed help, urgently.

When I saw mama and baby, I simply melted. The hedgehog was just beautiful. A little four-hundred-gram creature (African hedgehogs are smaller) with a white nose and two sugar eyes. She was a little pink squirt with short spines, like a toothbrush. She was the portrait of boundless suffering, at the end of her rope. Yet when her baby came near, she found the strength to rub its nose with her own and lick it. Slow and sweet. The image of maternal love. Then the hoglet nuzzled around for her nipples, looking for milk. From nipples to nose, nose to nipples.

I was sorry for all that hedgehog's pain. And, just as many other times, I couldn't find any sense in it. It truly pained me. That mama hedgehog's blood seemed like the blood of all the innocent creatures in this world.

I sprang into action. Hemostatic. Antibiotic. Hydration IV. Calcium. And then I called the Vale Wildlife Hospital. I described the situation in minute detail, and they told me it was very serious, but that the hedgehog could possibly be saved by surgery. Possibly.

So I called a colleague who handled exotic animals and brought the hedgehog to him.

"I'm not sure she'll be able to endure the operation, given her state. But if we leave her like she is, there's no hope," he said.

153

"Let's try the surgery," I decided.

I assisted. In that tiny belly, we made an incision just over a centimeter. We extracted the uterus. A retained placenta was the cause of the hemorrhage and the infection. The hedgehog was completely monitored, and everything went well. Once the operation was over, we left her under the oxygen mask for a while. She woke up slowly. When she started to move, I put her hoglet next to her. She licked its little head.

I hugged my fellow vet. We did it! We were elated.

Ten minutes after our explosion of joy, the little hedgehog gagged a couple of times. And within seconds, she was dead.

The image of that baby hedgie curled up to its dead mother stayed with me.

My return home was colored black. I buried the hedgehog under a centuries-old olive tree in the yard. That's where I bury all the hedgehogs that die. And the olive blooms every spring.

All I could do was take care of the orphaned hoglet. It was a little girl. I called her Carolina. She weighed nine grams.

Nine grams. A rosebud weighs more.

"Carolina, you won't end up like your mother. I'll do my best. I won't make any mistakes. And you'll be saved," I promised.

The following day, I had a doctor's appointment with a specialist in Milan. I couldn't change it, so I decided to take the hoglet with me. With all the necessary precautions, of course. I prepared a portable nursery, complete with food. A thermos to heat it up. And two hot water bottles to make sure she had the right temperature. One I would use right away, and before it cooled down, I would stop at a café for some hot water to fill the spare. After several stops, I finally reached Milan. I parked right in front of the medical building. I didn't like leaving Carolina in the car alone, but I had no alternative.

I was early, but I already needed a change of hot water. I took the empty water bottle and rang the buzzer. "Third floor," an anonymous voice said. I went up and entered that office, which was so luxurious I felt intimidated. I was greeted by a formal, rather haughty secretary. The mannered half-smile she gave me turned into a bewildered look when I showed her the water bottle and asked for some hot water. She directed me to the bathroom.

I was just coming out when a door opened. The medical luminary I was supposed to meet with was showing a patient out. He was impressive. Very tall. He saw me. I felt like I was at school, dealing with the most demanding, strict teachers. He raised his left eyebrow. Pointedly. He looked at me and then the hot water bottle. His eyes opened wider, forming a question mark. I felt obliged to offer an explanation.

"I . . . I . . . I have an appointment . . . an appointment with you. For an exam. But I have a . . . a . . . little animal in my car," I sputtered.

"A little animal?"

"A hedgehog."

"A hedgehog?"

He was like my echo, and he was only becoming more per-plexed.

He was sizing me up.

"Uh, yeah. A baby. But it's a long story. Maybe when it's my turn, I'll tell you about it," I said.

There. I'd made my usual impression as a—to put it mildly—strange character!

My turn came two and a half hours later. In the meantime, I'd checked on Carolina six or seven times.

"Good morning, Professor," I said.

"Good morning. Now will you explain?"

He'd been curious that whole time!

"I'm a veterinarian. I work with cattle. However . . . " I began, and I told him briefly about Ninna and the others. And Carolina and her mama. And this big, authoritative man melted. He was touched. And he asked me questions. He wanted to know, to understand.

"I'm a little worried because Carolina is in the car," I concluded.

"No! Bring her up!"

I ran to get her.

"She's a wonderful little thing," the luminary said.

Fortunately, the exam went well. Before letting me go, he

told the secretary, "Special discount for the vet. He's got a child to raise." We said good-bye, laughing.

I was hungry. I picked up a couple of vegan sandwiches and parked in a little alley that had a view of the Duomo and the piazza. And there, I ate my two sandwiches, admiring all that beauty with the little hedgie sleeping peacefully beside me. A drop of happiness.

29

Despite all her struggles, Carolina grew. Now she weighed fifty grams. She was extraordinary and very sweet. She called me with a particular cry. A tiny *pih, pih, piiih*. That little voice of hers was delightful.

One night a snowstorm broke out. It raged fiercely for most of the night. At a certain point, the electricity went out. It came back on right away, but then went out again. In that back-and-forth, the boiler quit working. And there was no getting it going again. The house rapidly got cold. Too cold. I panicked because I was afraid for Carolina. Such a low temperature was extremely dangerous for her. I got an electric heater and put it in the room where she was. As soon as the power came back, I turned it on. Meanwhile, outside, the snow had reached over three feet.

The next morning, Carolina's breathing was faster. And

she was a little colder. I gave her an antibiotic. But in the days that followed, the little thing worsened. I asked every expert I could reach for help. But the situation didn't turn. One morning she called me: *pih, pih, piiih* . . . I ran to her. "Carolina, are you hungry? I'll get your food right now." I picked her up as I spoke. But I realized immediately that she was letting go.

And so, in an instant, right there in my hands, she expired. I dropped down on a chair, burdened with a sharp, boundless grief. "I didn't want you to end up like your mother, I didn't want you to," I murmured.

It wasn't fair.

I felt a tremendous burden of guilt. Whether I was right or not, that didn't bring the hoglet back to life.

I buried her much later. Next to her mama. With some lavender. Over the earth that covered her, I placed a heart-shaped stone. A shield for her.

All around, almost without end, bright-white snow.

On Sundays Greta and I often went to see Daniela. She was sick. She had been for fifteen years. She was sick even when she'd organized that trip to Australia. Cancer. Sometimes it seemed to have gone away, but then it would come back.

Daniela had always given me moral support with my plan for the center. She enthusiastically approved everything I did. She loved animals. And all of nature. And she had a deep respect for it. She was such a radiant and intelligent and wise person. She was like a sister to me.

Her illness had come back and this time had metastasized to her lungs.

My dear friend's condition was very serious and made us fear the worst.

When we went to see her, I'd tell her about the hedgehogs to distract her. She listened attentively, with a faint smile. But she struggled to speak. She needed what little strength she had left to breathe.

She was suffering greatly. The burden of my sorrows was increased by the terrible torment of seeing her that way.

I didn't tell her Carolina was dead. I didn't want to make her any more upset.

One Sunday I brought her a picture of the African hoglet, along with a hundred others, because she was helping me to organize Hedgehog Day. I showed it to her, and she parted her lips to say something. But she couldn't. Daniela stayed with her mouth half-open for a while. With her voice not coming out. So she spoke with her eyes, telling me that Carolina touched her heart. Then, very slowly, she reached out and set the picture on her nightstand so she could see it whenever she wanted.

As Greta and I left, I lingered before closing the door behind me. I turned around, and my eyes met Daniela's. She was looking at me with infinite sweetness. I lingered a moment to return the gaze. A look full of kind words. And hugs. And heartfelt whispers: Don't be afraid . . . I to her and she to me. Moments of enormous intensity, saturated with emotion. Eyes that did not want to part, ever. We could both feel that we were saying good-bye for the last time.

Greta and I silently headed to the car. It was late. The moon, unmindful of human despair, shone in the dark of a cloudless sky. At that so difficult moment, I couldn't bear that great beauty. It clashed with my sadness.

We got home and went right to bed. But I couldn't fall asleep. I kept tossing and turning fitfully with my mind on Daniela. It was almost dawn when the phone rang. It was on the nearby dresser.

Greta leapt up and ran to answer it. "Yes . . . " she said, and then she burst into tears. I went to her, and already I know. Between sobs, she confirmed, "Daniela's gone." I hugged her tight, trying to console her. And trying to soothe my own broken heart.

I closed my eyes and went to my sister-friend: "Hi, my dear Daniela. Wherever you are, or wherever you're going, take Carolina with you. And her mother, too. They're two defenseless little creatures. Do you want to take care of them?"

Maybe it was just my imagination, but I felt like she replied. Nothing moved in the room, but the wind chimes hanging nearby swayed with a timid ding-ding. It was like "Yes, Massimo . . . " A subtle vibration, fading into my thoughts. Lifting them up.

30

Hubbub. The center was full of excitement. Yes, because I wanted to share hedgehogs and their world, and sensitize as many people as possible, and create a playful moment, and gather aid. How could I squeeze all these objectives into one day? I had an idea: Hedgehog Day! What date should it be? I'd thought of February, when there's the least work to be done with the hedgies, and the choice came down to Sunday the 22nd. The organizational work had begun a few months earlier, but now we were almost there, and we were in full frenzy.

Greta, besides printing out lots of pictures of our hedgehogs, had also made postcards with sweet and funny sayings, bookmarks, posters, drawings, and figurines. All "hedgehog themed." All made by hand. She had really gone out of her way.

And she wasn't the only one. The other volunteers had, too. Together, we'd inspired one another's imaginations and compiled our energies. A very generous friend had offered a space at her bed and breakfast for the party and the lunch. The wife of a friend of mine who's a wedding planner took care of the catering and decorating with good taste and definite impact. Others added to the menu by bringing additional dishes and mountains of cookies (hedgehog shaped). We made a learning zone with informational panels and more photos of our hedgehogs and drawings done by a professional cartoonist. It was crazy, far beyond our expectations.

But that wasn't enough. I thought we needed something more to liven it up. Dario! Yes, I had to get in touch with my friend Dario. He had a band. I called him up, and the band agreed to come to the party, including the singer.

What else was left? A raffle with some nice prizes up for grabs? Perfect! But how would we get those prizes? It was the moment to be shameless and go knocking on a few doors. So I did. And I found more than I had hoped for. From a publishing house, I got books, magazines, kids' games. Innumerable treats from a world-famous chocolate company. Organic products from a food company. Fine wine from a prestigious winery (including forty bottles of Barolo!). And much more from many others. I, Greta, and all the volunteers were thrilled and extremely happy.

And then . . . boom. Everything came screeching to a halt.

Because Daniela died.

She died one week before February 22, and I didn't feel like throwing a party. I just couldn't do it.

But everything had already been set in motion. The invitations had already gone out, and a hundred people had RSVP'd. Families with children. How could I let them all down? And my hedgehogs needed help. Medicines, food, equipment—everything costs money. Daniela would have come to the party and made it even better. So I closed my eyes and spoke to her again: "Daniela, I'm going to have the party. And you'll be there, too. Because I'll take you with me."

On Saturday the 21st, during the night, it snowed copiously. A constant, silent flurry of thick, fat snowflakes. I was outside shoveling snow in the hedgehog pens, since I never let snow completely bury their houses or the paths leading up to them, and I thought that, with the weather, no one would come to Hedgehog Day. I shoveled, worried. Nothing but the sound of my shovel. My hands got so numb they hurt. But my discouragement was worse. I thought that the roads might be impassable. Lots of people probably wouldn't leave home. At dawn, the snowflakes became small and sparse. They danced erratically in the air. Then stopped. I didn't go to sleep, staying up getting the last things ready for the party nonetheless.

It was ten thirty in the morning when the owner of the bed and breakfast called, worried. "Massimo, help!"

"Oh God, what happened?" I asked, alarmed.

"You have to come over here," she said. "I'm full of people. I don't know where to put them! The whole world showed up!"

I rushed over. I couldn't believe it. Even with that terrible weather, everyone had come. Everyone. Except Greta and my mother. My mother due to her poor health. Greta had helped me to the very last minute, but had told me she wasn't going to come. Because of Daniela.

The party began. And it was just wonderful. My father was among the guests. My cousin Francesco had come by as well. And there were friends. And the volunteers. And lots of strangers who then weren't strangers anymore. I needed to speak to all of them, and I'd never had such a large audience. I panicked for a moment. I'd written a good speech, but at the last minute decided to speak off the cuff.

I began by greeting and thanking everyone, then continued. "Today, my friend Daniela was supposed to be here with me." I said that in reality, she was, because I carried her in my heart. I told them about her, about her enthusiasm for my work with hedgehogs, about her love for nature. Then I talked about the center, about Ninna, Carolina, Jo, and all the others. In the hall, only my voice, occasionally breaking with emotion.

When I finished, there was a shower of applause, and it was then that I noticed all the people with wet eyes, veiled with tears. Patrizia—she had come with her whole family—was fearlessly, uncontrollably crying and at the same time passing tissues to everyone around her. My father came up to me a few moments later. "Good job, Massimo. You gave a proper speech. It was moving. From the heart, from yours to everyone else's here." What a feeling to hear those words from him. I'll never forget it.

Dario's band started up, and their notes, accompanied by the lead singer's mellifluous voice, wafted through the room. The party went off well, culminating in a huge cake with chocolate frosting. Which, sure enough, was in the shape of a hedgehog. I put a candle on top. It was also Susanna's birthday—she was with us, too—and it seemed right to surprise her with that gesture.

The inaugural Hedgehog Day, safe to say, was a smashing success.

Then there was the second one. Did it live up to the first? No . . . it topped it! Same atmosphere, fantastic decorations, the finest partners, and a really fun treasure hunt outside, since the weather permitted it. That all-around beautiful and productive day, we also freed some birds that had been rescued by the Wildlife Recovery Center in Cuneo. Their soaring into flight was pure poetry for us all.

The third Hedgehog Day was a real celebration. I had to find a bigger location, because the guest list got longer every time. We chose a movie theater space with a large stage. How we transformed that room! We plastered the walls with photos, drawings, and posters. We set up four long tables with hedgehog-embroidered tablecloths. Bowls with floating candles all around. And off in the back, an elegant counter with giveaways, flyers, and pamphlets.

Tons of food: ten dishes, all strictly vegan. And to liven things up? An excellent performer—both magician and comedian. But not just him, also two prizewinning tango dancers. And a lounge singer. Her father played soft piano to accompany her sweet, warbling voice. And we also showed an interesting documentary about hedgehogs in the afternoon.

I was satisfied. You couldn't ask for a better Hedgehog Day! Yet...

Yet there was something else. I had recently taken in Lisa, a hoglet with multiple problems. She was a fragile, sweet darling. I brought her with me, to the third Hedgehog Day, because I had to feed her periodically. She couldn't eat on her own. Volunteers and friends were abreast of the situation, and they helped me set her up in a small service bathroom. It was heated, and she would be comfortable in there.

The party was at its peak when I snuck away to check on her. The room was very cramped. A toilet and a small sink fit just barely. I took Lisa and a syringe with a little food and, sitting on the toilet—there was nowhere else—I started feeding her.

At that point, someone knocked on the door. "Someone's in here," I yelled, irritated. A small chorus of voices replied, almost in a whisper, "We don't need the bathroom. We want to see Lisa!" Darn! Someone, between friends and volunteers, had let the secret slip. It's not that I didn't want people to see her; I just couldn't allow her to be disturbed. It could make her anxious or stressed.

"I'm feeding her right now, and unfamiliar faces might scare her," I replied, worried.

"We'll be totally quiet. We really want to see her," the chorus insisted.

"Well . . . if you don't make any noise, if you keep your voices down, if you don't come all the way in, if you don't move . . . "

I was still giving out instructions, almost resigned, when the door slowly opened and several heads appeared: smiling, amazed faces. Fascinated, they murmured, "Hi, Lisa." Slightly embarrassed by my inelegant position, I wanted to say something. But I didn't bother. They were all there, motionless, silent. Captivated by the hedgehog. Ecstatic. Afterward, they said to me, "The best thing about today was seeing Lisa. Her eyes are sweet like an angel's."

That's how far we've come, to our third Hedgehog Day. I and all the people who gave their wonderful, effective help together. Because there is strength in unity. But in the future, there will be many, many more fantastic days like these.

31

L
ittle Lisa, who had won over all the guests at the third
Hedgehog Day with her angelic eyes, actually only had
one working eye. But she used it with such grace that you
didn't even notice the other. I met her in the month of Novem-
ber. A colleague called because a hedgehog had been brought
to his office. "It seems like it's dying, and I don't know how to
help it," he told me. He was right—just being a vet doesn't
mean you know how to treat hedgehogs. Academic preparation
isn't enough to take proper care of them. I had figured this out
myself after Ninna came into my life.

I rushed over to my colleague's. The hedgehog was in the
exam room. I opened the door and saw the tiny creature lying
on its side on the table, one of those all-steel ones. Not even a

towel between the hedgehog and the frigid metal. An unpleasant sense of cold came over me. I went over, thinking the hedgehog was dead—it was too still. But it was still breathing, just almost imperceptibly, very slowly. It opened one little eye, and at the same time, lifted its head a little. It stayed like that, observing me, for a few seconds.

All the world's melancholy was contained in its gaze.

I took the hedgehog and brought it home. It was a girl. I decided to call her Lisa, a name that seemed as sweet as she was. I examined her meticulously and gave her the treatment she needed. But as always, along with medical attention, I handled her in such a way as to transmit calm and affection. Then I prepared a water-sugar solution with a few drops of vanilla-flavored vitamin B, every so often brushing it lightly over her dry mouth to give her a little relief. I stayed by her side the whole night. Just twenty-four hours later, she showed signs of improvement, and it was then that she lifted her head again and looked at me. Like the day before, but longer. She even raised one of her front legs.

It seemed like she was reaching toward me.

I grabbed her extended little paw with two fingers.

An instant.

In the deep silence of the house, that intense contact filled up the room. It was like Lisa was holding on to my index finger.

I hadn't expected that.

It's a moment I'll never forget.

Lisa was paralyzed on one side from a trauma. One side was fine, the other was immobile, with a half-closed eye and drooping mouth. When she balled up, she couldn't close well: Her front legs touched her tail, her back legs her nose. Poor baby! I'd never seen a case like it. It was very serious. I asked myself a lot of questions, as I had other times before. Like with Salvo. But it was hard to think of euthanasia after the way Lisa had gripped my hand with her good front paw.

She was unable to eat on her own. She even had trouble swallowing. It took me hours and hours to feed her. The days were filled with ups and downs like a seesaw: One day she gained weight and I was happy, the next day she had gone down and I was sad. A constant battle. "Lisa, will you be here tomorrow?" I asked her every time. Hanging on by a thread, she went on. She endured. But for how long? Would she make it to Christmas, a holiday celebrating love? After that, to January? And to Hedgehog Day, my big day? That's how it was with her: all frighteningly uncertain.

Meanwhile, I found out that she had a horrible parasite and had begun treatment. When Lisa's appetite diminished drastically, I was overwhelmed with despair. A volunteer from the center helped me. "Massimo, I gave my hedgie chicken. She loved it! Why don't you try giving Lisa some?"

"Hah! I don't think it's as appetizing as the wet cat food I offer her. But I'd like to give it a try," I told her.

I made poached chicken, which I blended with a little broth to make a smooth puree. I added some vitamins and pulled the mixture into a syringe. I brought it to Lisa's mouth. Her head lurched back. She didn't want it. Then the miracle happened. I wish I had filmed it. She began, as much as she was capable, going after the syringe. Overtaken by an uncontainable euphoria. She liked it.

She started gaining weight and doing better. The other volunteers and I prepared a very special box for her. Three feet by three feet, in heavy wood and well-padded inside, so that even when she moved in her own particular way, rolling or falling, she wouldn't hurt herself. A fantastic box.

Except.

We hadn't padded the outside as well, alas, and one night when I was running barefoot to pick up the phone, I stumbled right over the corner. A disaster. I broke my pinky toe. The pain! My foot was swollen, the toe black and blue. But I didn't go to the emergency room. I didn't have time. I treated it myself.

Meanwhile, one thing after another was going on at the center. For example, several TV shows came to film the hedgehogs and our activities, and I had to do interviews. I was happy because that all meant major publicity and awareness raising. But I had more work to do with the hedgehogs, and I started to feel a deep physical tiredness. Besides that, I didn't sleep much and only ate when I had time. On several occasions, I'd felt like I was about to faint, but one evening it was worse.

I lay down in bed and listened to my heart's odd rhythm: No, this was not okay. Plus I had a constant tingling in my left arm. And chest pain.

Well, I could explain the chest pain. I'd fallen a month before. I had seen a small cat in the middle of the road and stopped to avoid hitting it. He sprang toward the cherry tree and climbed up a fence, past which were stacks of road signs and street repair equipment. It was cold, and I was worried about that kitty. I tried to get to him so I could take him and help him. But he got scared and quickly slipped between the piles of junk and got away from me. What could I do? I passed by every evening, jumped over the gate, and left him a little food. He studied me with his emerald eyes from hiding spots I couldn't get to. Then I left. When I was a ways away, I looked and saw that he came out and ate.

During one of those jumps, I slipped on the ice, and my chest slammed against the top of the gate. An unbelievable pain. I even had trouble breathing. But that was awhile ago. Could the pain I felt now in my sternum be linked to that blow? Maybe? No.

I was concerned. Meanwhile, night had fallen and it seemed like the symptoms were becoming more acute. I called my friends Claudio and Luisa. I'd met them at the second Hedgehog Day. Wonderful people. He worked as a nurse in a cardiac intensive care unit. He would surely be able to give me some advice.

He didn't even let me finish. Alarmed, he said right away, "Massimo, you need to call 911."

"But if they take me to the hospital, who's going to take care of the hedgehogs? Who'll feed Lisa?" I replied, distressed.

"We'll handle it, Luisa and I. You know Luisa is the only person besides you able to feed Lisa," he reassured.

I phoned a volunteer, whose name was also Luisa—an invaluable profusion of Luisas that night! She lived nearby and could give me a hand. She, bless her heart, came right over, even though it was 11 p.m. Then I called 911. As I was waiting for the ambulance, still in my pajamas, I dragged myself to the computer and drafted a detailed map of the positions of all the hedgehogs, my full little hospital. And for each hedgehog, I specified their treatments, habits, and type and quantity of food. I painstakingly reviewed it all. Even if I felt terrible, I hadn't lost my sense of humor—I added a title in large font: "In the Event of My Death." An unusual will, no? It made me smile, thinking of someone reading those instructions.

Then I began, laboriously, feeding Lisa. At least she wouldn't go hungry. She was so fragile. And that's how the paramedics found me. They looked upon the scene in puzzlement. A half-dead man with a pale, haggard face, in pajamas and a pained look, feeding a hedgehog; and Luisa, my volunteer, grumbling, annoyed, that she had told me to lie down, but I wouldn't listen.

They said they'd seen some strange things, but nothing like that. They immediately did several tests on me, as I broadly explained the situation with my hedgehogs that needed me, and I also told them, succinctly, about my symptoms. They ascertained that I wasn't having a heart attack, but they had to take me to the hospital for some additional tests. "Well, if I'm not dying, I'll just go myself tomorrow," I said. Satisfied, they left.

A few minutes later, Claudio called me. He and his wife were on their way over. "Actually, you need to go to the hospital now. The heart's not one to mess around with," Claudio told me, adamant.

My friends met me there. Claudio stayed with me. The two Luisas went to my house—I hadn't been able to attend to all the hedgehogs, so they would take care of it. Luisas, the Wonder Women!

At the hospital, they began testing. I remember thinking, "Well, I'm here, and here I must stay. I might as well take the opportunity to rest a little." I fell asleep instantly. A long, deep sleep. I needed it.

I was released about twenty-four hours later. The doctors didn't find anything serious, fortunately. Happy—and rested—I returned to my hedgehogs. The first thing I did was hug Lisa with abandon. "Little one! Did you know I almost died before you? And yet here we are, both of us!" Claudio and the two Luisas were indispensable and extraordinary. Some friends, right? I can never thank them enough.

When I wasn't feeling well, before calling them, for a moment I'd thought of asking Greta for help.

But.

But between me and her, gradually, things had changed. We weren't a couple anymore. It just happened, without us realizing it. Great affection and friendship were still there. Still, I didn't feel like calling her. Plus, she lived too far away.

Life went on. And Lisa is still here with me. She was sponsored by a girl who works in a foreign country and writes poems for her, saying that Lisa has more points than a rose's thorns, yet in comparison is more beautiful. She calls Lisa the "ancient warrior of the woods" and the "little gift made of love."

For me, too, Lisa is a great little gift.

Every single moment with her is precious, because it could be the last.

And this terrible truth makes me see clearly how precarious everything and everyone is.

And the beauty of every instant.

That's why I want to live every moment without wasting any time.

And stopping to embrace the little warrior of the woods has infinite meaning.

32

Where could my little Ninna be? In what corner of the woods is she smiling up at the moon? And when the dawn comes, does my baby hoglet, anticipating the notes of the first morning bird, run nimbly to her nest?

Is she full or hungry?

Is she thirsty?

Or cold?

Does she remember me?

Will I see her again one day?

Frequently—and as soon as I notice, I correct myself—I accidentally call Lisa "Ninna." Well, Ninna is always in my heart. I know, I often fall into humanizing her too much, my Ninna, and sometimes I go over the top. I treated her like a daughter. And I thought that keeping her and protecting her was an act of love. I realized only later, and after much struggle, that love is also understanding, accepting, and respecting another being's nature. And that true love doesn't ask for anything in return.

Every hedgehog that has come through the center, or is still here, is in my heart, too. Because each has left a mark. I recognize Ninna in the eyes of every one of them.

She is all hedgehogs. And all hedgehogs are Ninna.

That unkempt little hoglet fell at my feet, which had been wandering in a certain direction three years ago. It was the right time, because I think that you only consider and pursue a certain path when you're ready. Ninna triggered so many changes that it feels like centuries have passed since that May. First of all, I've changed. No, on second thought, that's not quite it—more than "changed," I found myself again. I found that part of myself that was repressed and well-hidden. That was waiting for Ninna to burst out.

No more frills or vanity, but rediscovered values.

The value of life. Of love. Of helping out.

Hedgehogs are protected animals. They are at risk of extinction.

But that's definitely not the only reason I work with them.

The meaning of my help, even if what I do is just a drop in the ocean, is related to compassion, a word that comes from *cum* (together) and *patior* (to suffer). Compassion as suffering with another, participating in that suffering. This is the first point, followed by a desire to compensate for harm done by others, those who accidentally hit or injure a hedgehog.

Or for those who don't even consider it.

Anyway, what's a hedgehog compared to the world? A very, very tiny dot?

Well, changing our point of view, I could also ask: What is our world compared to our galaxy? A very, very tiny dot.

So is it just our perspective that, enveloped in the limited realities that pertain to us, makes anything more or less relevant?

The fact is that we're in an immense universe where, in my opinion, everything is important, because in the end, every creature—and I stress, *every creature*—forms part of a marvelous harmony that has to be protected.

But it's not due to a question of dots and angles that I take care of hedgehogs.

I take care of them—here it is again—out of love.

Love is what gives sense to life.

Immersed in the work of my little hospital, I trouble myself to alleviate the suffering of tired, poor, huddled hedgehogs and try to give them back a piece of existence they would otherwise be denied. There you have it—you have to involve the heart. In every act. I so wish that this passion of mine were like a highly contagious virus that spread as widely as possible and sparked good feelings all around.

That way everyone would do something to help others, be they hedgehogs, kids, old people, or trees. If everyone did our part, these drops of water, all together, would form oceans. And a better world.

Ninna's voice is that of all nature outraged by man.

It's the cry of a leveled forest.

It's the lament of tortured biodiversity.

It's the mass rebuke of pirates who unrestrainedly prey on an already violated planet.

It's the scream that wants to shake indifference.

It's the call for help that we should all listen to. So that all our lives can continue.

I'm not interested in having big houses and nice cars and seeing what I can get away with. That's not my idea of happiness. I just want to keep chasing my dreams, which have no more restraints. And catch them in their gardens. And make them blossom. So I can give them away.

My dreams respond to Ninna's voice.

Ninna, my first little hedgehog. I never saw her again.

EPILOGUE

This book ends here, whereas the story of my hedgehogs and the center goes on.

Every once in a while, at night, I go to that plot of land I bought near Susanna's Paradise, another paradise.

I sit on that grass teeming with life, on the edge of the woods, and call out, "Ninna, Ninnaaa . . . " And on certain magical nights, the kind stolen from fairy tales, she is carried to me on a breeze. When the trees open up to the wind's caress, somehow, she arrives. Soft, like the music of the angels, for my heart.

ACKNOWLEDGMENTS

To Mother and Father—yes, I first want to thank them both. For all the love and help they've always given me. I know they're constantly worried about me, and I'm sorry about that. They're concerned about my health, because I spend all my time and energy on my hedgehogs, neglecting sleep and food. Well, they're not entirely wrong; I know I can be extreme, but this is the path I've chosen and that satisfies my spirit. If my body suffers a little, so be it. Franchina and Mario, I'm telling you here: Don't get too worked up . . .

A special thanks to my cousin Francesco, who constantly helps with my hedgehogs and who is a guardian angel to my Franchina.

I want to thank Remigio Luciano, who helped me to start

the La Ninna Hedgehog Rescue Center, a division of the Cuneo Wild Animal Rescue Center, which he founded. I also thank him for his help and ongoing support. For more information on his rescue center, go to: www.centrorecuperoselvatici.it.

I thank Dorthe Madsen for her precious advice. She is my living encyclopedia on hedgehogs and their world! We have a strong friendship, bound by a great love for nature—hedgehogs included—and a deep mutual affection. Dorthe directs the Pindsvinenes Håb Recovery Center in Tranbjerg, Denmark.

Thanks to Giulia Paracchini and Gérard Mangiagalli. Under Giulia's precise guidance, I was able to get started. She was essential! And I have always turned to Gérard for the more complicated cases that come to the center. Gérard is a member of, and Giulia is vice president of, Milano Natura, an association that has been working to help hedgehogs and other animals for years. For more information on the association, see: www.milanonatura.it (the site includes rescue assistance for people who find hedgehogs).

Thanks to Susanna and all my dear friends, who all support me in different ways. And among them, particular thanks to Enrico for the captivating photo spread he did on my hedgehogs. And to photographer Bruno Murialdo, who captures emotion with his shots.

Thanks to Andrea Brovida, without whom I'd never have met my Ninna!

Another very special thanks to all the wonderful volunteers who take turns helping at the center—they're beyond indispensable.

And I want to thank Antonella Tomaselli. We met one day, on the same wavelength, and easily became friends. She listened to the story of me and my hedgehogs and, with her magical and subtle pen, turned it into this book.